HOW TO DOWNLOAD THE WALKING EYE APP

Available on purchase of this guide only.

1. Visit our website: www.insightguides.com/walkingeye
2. Download the Walking Eye container app to your smartphone (this will give you access to your free eBook and the ability to purchase other products)
3. Select the scanning module in the Walking Eye container app
4. Scan the QR Code on this page – you will be asked to enter a verification word from the book as proof of purchase
5. Download your free eBook* for travel information on the go

* Other destination apps and eBooks are available for purchase separately or are free with the purchase of the Insight Guide book

CONTENTS

ART LOVERS

Choose route 8 to visit artsy Holualoa on Hawai'i Island, or route 1, Honolulu, for the Hawai'i Art Museum and architectural delights of Honolulu.

RECOMMENDED ROUTES FOR...

ESCAPING WAIKIKI

Don't be a visitor who never leaves — try routes 2 and 3 to see the best of Oahu — including the country.

FAMILIES

Children will love Aulani (route 4) and the beaches of routes 2 and 3, which hop from swimming hole to shave ice along the coast of Oahu.

HISTORY BUFFS

Hawai'i has a rich history — both pre-Western contact and during World War II. Route 5 is best for Hawaiiana, and route 4 takes you to Pearl Harbor.

ISLAND HOPPING

Up for a day trip? Consider flying to any of the neighbor islands – routes 6, 9 and 15 work best for maximum sightseeing with limited time.

NATURAL HAWAI'I

West Kauai (route 11) and Volcanoes National Park (route 10) showcase Hawai'i's geological roots best. Science and nature fans will also enjoy Hilo (route 9).

SEASIDE FUN

For the best beaches, those that dot Hawai'i's coast like pink crescents, follow routes 2, 11 and 15 around Oahu, Kauai and Maui respectively.

SHOPPING

Shoppers will delight in routes 1 and 4 – the best shopping in Hawai'i all happens on Oahu.

INTRODUCTION

An introduction to Hawai'i's geography, customs and culture, plus illuminating background information on cuisine, history and what to do when you're there.

Waikiki Beach

EXPLORE HAWAI'I

On the six major, freely visitable islands of Hawai'i, spectacular scenery, colorful history and modern comforts add up to paradise.

Aloha! Get used to hearing it – the *aloha* spirit of hospitality and sharing – truly is felt in everything you will do while visiting Hawai'i. From the moment you land and are greeted with a *lei* at your hotel to the times you stray from the map and need a little assistance finding your way back, Hawai'i's residents paired with its climate and stunning geography make a trifecta that creates a perfect tropical adventure.

Hawai'i is officially the most remote group of islands in the world, thus there really is no better place to get away. The first tourists traveled for over a week to arrive via ship.

Today, Hawai'i is a unique blend of traditional Hawaiian culture and Western influence, making it unlike any other place in the world. The islands have become home to an amazingly diverse gathering of peoples from all over the world. These cultures have grown together, creating a new, distinctly Hawaiian take on food, fashion and art.

GEOGRAPHY/LAYOUT

The Hawaiian Islands are made up of eight main islands. From east to west: Hawai'i (commonly called the Big Island or Hawai'i Island), Maui, Kaho'olawe Lana'i, Moloka'i, O'ahu, Kaua'i and Ni'ihau. All but Kaho'olawe, once used for military target practice, are inhabited. Really, there are many, many more. The island chain stretches approximately 1,500 miles (2,400km) and includes 137 islands.

Transportation on all of the islands is almost exclusively by car, and on Oahu, traffic is a problem. Avoid highways at rush hour at all costs. While bus systems exist, they are unreliable, especially on the neighbor islands, as all islands except Oahu are often referred to. Walking in urban areas, like Waikiki and Honolulu, is always recommended when traveling short distances, as parking can be challenging.

Interisland travel is quick and easy via Hawaiian Air, however, since the loss of the airlines competitors Aloha Airlines and Go! Airlines, prices have sky-rockets as they run what is effectively a monopoly. Expect to pay a minimum of $80 each way for flights as short as 20 minutes, and be sure to look into the lesser-known Island Air, owned by Larry Ellison, who also now owns most of Lanai.

The morning sun peeks through lush vegetation along the Kalalau Trail

HISTORY

Hawai'i was colonized by Polynesians so many years ago that we can't even be sure – some studies show it was as far back 300 AD. Officially discovered, in the Western sense, by Captain James Cook in 1778, one thing everyone can agree upon: it's hard to imagine why anyone would ever want to leave. Cook named the archipelago the 'Sandwich Islands' in honor of the Earl of Sandwich, and opened the doors to the west. He was killed only a year later at Kealakekua Bay on Hawai'i Island.

King Kamehameha unified the Hawaiian Islands, formally establishing the Kingdom of Hawai'i in 1810 and preserved Hawai'i's independence under his rule. In 1820, the first Protestant missionaries arrived on Hawai'i Island. Hawai'i also became a port for seamen, traders and whalers. Throughout these years of growth, Western disease took a heavy toll on the Native Hawaiian population. Hawaiians, an isolated people, were unusually vulnerable to introduced diseases and smallpox, measles, Hansen's disease, whooping cough, influenza and gonorrhea, took their toll. By 1920, the estimated Hawaiian population of 200,000 pure Hawaiians numbered only 25,000 and their life expectancy was only 35 years.

In 1893, American Colonists who controlled much of Hawai'i's economy overthrew the Hawaiian Kingdom in a peaceful, yet controversial coup. In

Humpback Whales

Visit Hawai'i in the winter months, and you'll have company: the humpback whales will be here as well, having traveled from the cold Alaskan waters. Here to mate, give birth and nurture newborn, whales like privacy – federal law requires a 300ft (100-meter) distance for whale watchers. This is strictly enforced by arrest and fine, and occasionally jail.

You can see whales anywhere, even off Diamond Head, but your safest bet is in the sheltered waters between Maui, Molokai, Lanai and Kahoolawe. Don't worry about finding a whale-watching boat on Maui. They'll find you. The best are the Pacific Whale Foundation (www.pacificwhale.org) or Captain Nemo (http://scubashack.com) excursions, not exactly luxurious like the big boats, but sure to be an adventure. On Kauai, try Captain Andy's (www.napali.com) off of the west side.

Whale watching season is November through April, and sometimes they stay into May. They're not hard to find; you'll see them when they spout – inhaling and exhaling on the surface – and when they fluke, spy hop and breach. There are an estimated 600 whales in Hawai'i, a mere fraction of a century ago. You'll quickly realize that they're even bigger than you imagined: 10–15ft (3–4 meters) long at birth, weighing 1–3 tons (1,016–3,048kg). Newborns gain 200lbs (90kg) a day, and adults average 40 tons (40,642kg) in weight.

Local life in Haleʻiwa

Hawaiian Language

Until the 1970s, linguists agreed that the Hawaiian language stood little chance of survival. However, local people could be heard chattering in pidgin, a hybrid island language. A typical after-work conversation between people might include this: 'Hey, pau hana like go my hale for grind?' Translation: 'Hey, after work would you like to go to my house to eat?' Pidgin is interesting to hear, but don't try to emulate it – nothing makes locals laugh harder.

Today, pidgin dominates among locals, but true Hawaiian is increasingly heard among part-Hawaiian members of many families and other individuals. The change is credited to a renaissance of pride in being Hawaiian and establishment of immersion schools, where all classes are taught in the native language. Today, not only children take classes to ʻolelo (speak) Hawaiian, their parents do too, in order to keep up with their multilingual kids. There are Hawaiian language courses offered in high schools and as a major at University of Hawaiʻi.

Every letter in Hawaiian is pronounced distinctly. Vowels have just one sound: *a* sounds like *ah*, *e* like *ay*, *i* like *ee*, *o* like *oh*, and *u* like *oo*. Likelike Highway, for example, is correctly pronounced *lee-kay lee-kay*, not *like-like*. Glottal stops, called ʻokina, indicate that each vowel should be pronounced distinctly.

1898, Hawaiʻi became a territory of the United States. Queen Liliʻuokalani was imprisoned in Iolani Palace. On December 7, 1941, the Japanese launched a surprise attack on Pearl Harbor on Oahu, and four years later, on September 2, 1945, Japan signed its unconditional surrender on the USS Battleship *Missouri*, which still rests in Pearl Harbor today. In 1959, Hawaiʻi became the 50th State of the United States. Statehood is still controversial – many native Hawaiians believe the annexation was unlawful and should be reversed or, at least, made amends for.

CLIMATE

Hawaiʻi's climate includes mild temperatures year-round, moderate humidity and persistant northeasterly winds called the tradewinds. Hawaiʻi experiences great variations in rainfall over relatively short distances. Take Kauai, for example, with Mount Waiʻaleʻale, the wettest place on earth, getting an average of 45ins (11,430mm) of rain per year. Just down the road, not more than 20 miles (32km) away as the crow flies, Poipu receives less than 20ins (500mm) of rain per year. It's best to always have an umbrella handy, as rains often come on quickly on otherwise sunny and clear days.

Ocean temperatures vary from a low of 73–74°F (23°C) in the winter months to a high near 80°F (27°C) during the summer months – always comfortable for swimming, surfing and diving.

Bakery in Wailuku

Haleakala Crater seen from the Hana Highway

POPULATION

The majority of Hawai'i's 1.2 million people live on the island of Oahu, which includes the state capital, Honolulu. With more than 800,000 residents, this is truly a bustling urban center. The population is often referred to as 'a melting pot' due to the great cultural diversity found in Hawai'i. The Hawaiians were joined by many eastern cultures, including the Japanese, Chinese and Korean immigrants to work on sugar plantations in the late 19th and early 20th century. Other immigrants came from Portugal, Europe, and now, as a state of the United States, there is truly a little bit of every culture here in Hawai'i.

Neighbor islands are significantly less crowded. Hawai'i Island has approximately 150,000 residents, Maui has 115,000, Kauai has 58,000, Molokai has 7,400, Lanai 3,000 and Ni'ihau 160.

DON'T LEAVE HAWAI'I WITHOUT

Watching the sunrise from the top of Haleakala. The Hawaiians called this place the house of the sun for a reason. You'll feel like you woke up with the sun – because you did – and will be blown away by the beauty of Maui.

A surfing lesson in Waikiki. Surfing is Hawai'i's gift to the world, and you can master it in an hour with the help of a local expert. There's no safer or more picturesque place to learn than from the Waikiki beach boys in the lee of Diamond Head.

Learning about Hawai'i's important role in World War II. Hawai'i's fame as a tourist destination rose in part because it was the first glimpse of home for many returning servicemen during the war. It's role in the war was great, and the USS *Arizona* is the place to see it first-hand.

Eating a plate lunch. Made up of meat, rice and 'mac' salad, the plate lunch is Hawai'i's version of a deli-sandwich for lunch. Any roadside 'Drive In' will have one – and you must try it once.

Visiting Bishop Museum. Hawai'i's rich culture and history is unlike anything you're apt to experience again and there's no better or more beautiful place to experience it than Bishop Museum. Learn all about the volcanoes that made up this island chain there too.

Taking a whale-watching or snorkeling tour. Getting out on the water is a must – the islands are most beautiful when looking back at the coast. There are tours on every island and durations that will work for all.

Having a sunset cocktail on the beach. It's unlikely anyone needs to be told – but just in case, choose from one of the many waterfront dining options, park yourself at 6pm, and just watch the sun sink with a Mai Tai in hand.

Meeting the locals. Hawai'i's people are welcoming, kind and excited to share their home with visitors. Ask questions anywhere you go – you'll find the people are friendlier here than anywhere else in the world.

CUSTOMS AND ETIQUETTE

Hawai'i's customs have roots in many different cultures as a result of the state's great diversity. In Hawai'i, you never, ever wear your shoes into someone's home. At a party, you'll see piles of 'slippers' – what local people call flip-flops or thongs – piled at the door. It's local custom to always bring a gift and food is the gift of choice.

In Hawai'i, it's normal to celebrate Girls' Day, Boys' Day, Prince Kuhio Day and St. Patrick's Day. All public holidays are a reason to take time off work and relax with family and friends – usually at the beach.

The exchange of *lei* (flower garlands) is perhaps Hawai'i's best-known custom. You'll likely be welcomed at your hotel with a *lei* upon check-in. In general, they are given by local people to friends, family and colleagues to celebrate birthdays, promotions or sometimes for no reason at all – just because. The *lei* is always put on the recipient, and in most instances, given with a kiss on the cheek, although men tend not to do so when giving other men *lei*. It's not proper to hand someone their *lei*, nor to put one on yourself.

POLITICS AND ECONOMICS

Hawai'i's political landscape reflects its many cultures – there is a wide variety of political beliefs throughout the state. Traditionally a democratic state, Hawai'i voted largely in favor of President Obama, a local boy and Punahou graduate, for US president in the 2008 elections.

The state's constitution was drafted in 1950 and came into effect when Hawai'i became a state in 1959. The diversity of the state has led to the first Filipino Governor of an American state – Ben Cayetano in 1994, one of few republican leaders elected in Hawai'i, and more recently, Tulsi Gabbard, the first American Samoan and first Hindu member of the United States Congress. Hawai'i has two representatives and two senators in the United States Congress, and four electoral votes.

Economically, Hawai'i faces challenges and it is notoriously hard for small businesses and the middle classes to prosper. Real estate prices, combined with high prices on imported foodstuffs, put the cost of living among the nation's highest. Day-to-day living can be a struggle for local residents, but most wouldn't give up living in Hawai'i for the world.

A UNIQUE DESTINATION

You've chosen to come somewhere unlike anywhere else in the world – a unique mix of modern and tradition, a blend of cultures and geological beauty that is awe-inspiring. There are countless opportunities to learn about it all in the Best Routes section of this guide. Whether you prefer history, culture or surfing, there's truly something for everyone.

Hanalei Bay and the Emerald Mountains on the island of Kauai

TOP TIPS FOR EXPLORING HAWAII

Choose your island carefully. Selecting an island or two to visit can be difficult. Check out the populations section, and consider this: Kauai is the oldest island, so it's the steepest, greenest and most dramatic. Hawai'i Island is the newest and is vast, uncrowded and warm. Oahu is the population's center and is a bustling place with the most people, restaurants and nightlife. Maui has it all – things to do, beauty and a quieter pace. Molokai and Lanai are extremely quiet, and best for those looking to simply relax and do very little on vacation.

Protect your skin. Sunburn ruins many a Hawaiian vacation – all too many visitors think they'll just get a little sun on the first day, then learn that even 15 minutes in our sun can lead to a burn that causes pain, blistering and peeling for days. Be extra cautious – wear a hat daily and put sunscreen on before leaving the hotel, even if you're not going to the beach. Don't forget the tops of your feet!

Book trips in advance. Reservations for the USS *Arizona* can be made online up to two months in advance of your trip to avoid having to wait in line for same-day tickets. This will allow you to instead take the West Oahu tour, wrapping up with the memorial tour.

Book your hotel early. Accommodations vary greatly, both in price and in quality. The earlier you book at hotel, the better rate you'll get, as prices only increase in time. For a high value, consider the Outrigger family of resorts – there are many on each island. Focused on providing experiences that acquaint visitors with the local culture, this family-run resort chain was one of the first in Waikiki. Note: there are only seven oceanfront hotels in Waikiki – look closely for 'oceanfront' vs. 'near beach' to be sure – everything is near the beach in Hawai'i.

Shop local. Shopping in Waikiki can be an interesting experience. Many of the higher end stores cater to Japanese and Chinese visitors who are known to come to Hawai'i exclusively to shop and spend copious amounts. Local people are often completely ignored by salespeople, and if you look local, you may be as well. Little known tip – T Galleria, the duty-free shops located centrally in Waikiki, is a large center whose first two floors are open to everyone, not just international tourists. The beauty department is the largest in Hawai'i.

Get with the lingo. Directions are given strangely in Hawai'i. Expect to hear *mauka* and *makai*, Diamond Head and 'Ewa. *Mauka* means 'toward the mountains' and *makai* means 'toward the ocean'. Once you have a hang of it, it's quite easy, because you can always look around for the mountains. Diamond Head is used on Oahu only, for east, and 'Ewa for west.

Dim sum, Honolulu Chinatown

FOOD AND DRINK

With ethnic influences from Polynesia, Asia, Europe and North America Hawai'i's cuisine is among the world's most eclectic.

Hawaiian menus read like a United Nations lunch order: sushi, pasta, crispy *gau gee*, *kim chee*, tortillas, tandoori chicken, Wienerschnitzel, spring rolls – you name it, they eat it in Hawaii. Island restaurants span the gamut from roadside shack to swanky and formal. In between is everything from casual beachfront tiki bars to family-friendly diners and bistros. Within a relatively small geographical area, visitors find a universe of dishes served in surroundings both down-home and haute, from casual eateries that serve two scoops of rice for a 'plate lunch' to candlelit corners with chateaubriand and chocolate mousse on the menu.

Most of the time, the best restaurants are located in central commercial areas: on rare occasions, good restaurants will stand alone. It's common to find multiple cuisines clustered in one area. The exception is Honolulu's Chinatown, which boasts a preponderance of restaurants serving Asian food.

LOCAL CUISINE

The most recent take on island food is called Hawai'i Regional Cuisine – a variation of what's known elsewhere as Pacific Rim Cuisine or New Australian Cuisine. This movement gained momentum in 1992, when a dozen curious, creative and congenial chefs began getting together to share their ideas as well as their wish lists for a wider variety of fresh produce and other more varied ingredients.

The growth of Hawai'i Regional Cuisine has made a difference on Hawai'i's culinary scene. Today, any number of farmers are growing crops to the specifications of chefs who visit the fields and make known what they want for their own restaurants. Tomatoes are vine-ripened; arugula and baby lettuces fill upcountry fields on Maui and the Big Island. Several hotels grow their own fresh herbs, while a number of hotels in Waikiki have their own rooftop hydroponic gardens, and at least one Maui resort harvests fresh tropical fruit and other produce from an organic garden that surrounds its parking lot.

Hawaiian Regional Cuisine has become a palate-pleasing password even beyond island shores. Names such as Alan Wong, Sam Choy and Roy Yamaguchi, owners of several restau-

Desert at Mama's Fish House   *Sashimi platter*

rants who have published cookbooks and hosted their own television cooking shows, have become synonymous with Hawaiian cooking. The current greats include George Mavrothalassitis, Peter Merriman and Daniel Thiebaut, each with their own signature restaurants.

Hawai'i has many to thank for its tasty diversity. Chinese immigrants, for instance, taught islanders that rice goes just as well with eggs at breakfast as it does with lunch and dinner. Supermarkets stock supplies of *cilantro*, lemongrass and ginger, and restaurants turn out everything from Mandarin, Sichuan and Cantonese to Mongolian barbecue and stir-fry.

From the Japanese came the gifts of *shoyu* (soy sauce), *sashimi* (thinly sliced raw fish) and *tempura* (deep-fried vegetables and meats) and almost every street has a sushi bar. Thailand has introduced spring rolls, *mee krob* (noodle salad) and a coconut-milk/hot pepper-flavored dish called Evil Jungle Prince, best followed by Thai iced tea with sweetened condensed milk. Vietnamese food – less spicy than Thai – is particularly popular for its *phô*, a broth with noodles and beef or chicken slices. Portuguese influence makes itself known in *pao dolce* (sweet bread), sausage and a robust bean soup.

WHERE TO EAT

It's easy to eat well on the Hawaiian Islands. With a multitude of good res-

taurants serving up a bevy of different cuisines and there are options at every price point. If you're eating breakfast or lunch, reservations aren't necessary. For dinner, however, especially in some of the busier tourist spots such as Honolulu on Oahu and Lahaina or Paia on Maui, it's always a good idea to book a table in advance by phone or online.

Etiquette in Hawaiian restaurants is the same as it is in restaurants on the US mainland. Beach attire is generally acceptable for breakfast and lunch, but for dinner guests should spruce up a bit (read: no ballcaps or tank tops). Tipping servers also is customary; 15

For the love of spam

Spam has a special place in the Hawaiian diet; it is sometimes referred to as the 'Hawaiian Steak'. Residents of the islands consume more Spam per capita than any residents of any other place in the US. This popularity can be attributed in part to the military; in the years that followed World War II, the meat product was used as a substitute for fresh meat, and, gradually, surplus supply of it made its way into native diets. Today in the islands, the canned meat is most commonly eaten atop a rectangle of rice and bound with a piece of nori seaweed. The resulting sushi-like creation is called Spam musubi.

The Moana Surfrider beach bar

percent is standard for average service; good service deserves 20 percent. For restaurants, see page 98.

Sunset drinks and pupus

Sunset is a time to slow down, pull up a chair, and enjoy drinks and *pupus* (hors d'oeuvres). Nearly anywhere in Waikiki is good. Some of the best are at the Halekulani or the Sheraton Moana-Surf rider. The Halekulani's House Without a Key is a great place to enjoy Hawaiian music, hula and 'heavy pupus,' that can easily serve as dinner. On the western shores of all of the islands, you'll find similar venues, including Huggo's (Kona) and Hula Grill (Lahaina). On Kauai, head to the St. Regis at Princeville.

High-end restaurants

For fine dining, Alan Wong's on Oahu, just a few miles out of Waikiki, is the best. Reservations are required. Chef Mavro's French cuisine, Morimoto for the best Japanese food and presentation, and BLT in the Trump Hotel are also highly recommended. On Maui, Mama's Fish House is the best of both worlds – fine dining and ocean views, or Ko, in Wailea, for the best of Pacific Rim. On Kauai, consider Postcards at Hanalei, or Tidepools at the Grand Hyatt Poipu. If on a budget, consider instead going for lunch, but call ahead to ensure the restaurant is open.

Farmer's markets

For the best and freshest produce, explore some of the islands' farmers' markets. Not just for buying your produce, they all offer fresh meals as well. On Oahu, check out the People's Open Market in Honolulu, the Saturday market at the Kapiolani Community College on Diamond Head Road in Honolulu for breakfast and the Thursday market at Kailua Square Shopping Center in Kailua for dinner. On Maui, the Maui Swap Meet on Kahului Beach Road at Maui Community College is a great option. On Hawai'i Island, the Hilo Farmers' Market is great for fresh fruit (especially papaya). On Kauai, the Kauai Community Market goes off weekly on the campus of the local community college across from Grove Farm in Lihu'e.

Ethnic restaurants

Every town in Hawai'i is home to Japanese, Chinese and often, Vietnamese and Thai food as well. These are wonderful experiences for lunch and dinner. On Oahu or Maui, head to Sansei for the freshest sushi bar. Sit at the bar

---

Food and Drink Prices

Price categories are for a two-course meal, paired with a glass of wine, if served at the restaurant.

$ = less than $25
$$ = $25–50
$$$ = $50–75
$$$$ = $75 and up

Plate lunches   _Fruit stall at Hilo Farmer's Market_

and eat what the chef suggests for the best experience. Chinatown, on Oahu, offers the greatest number of Chinese restaurants. Little Village, a casual family-style restaurant, is the local favorite. Vietnamese _phô_ can be found in almost any strip mall in Hawai'i and Saeng's Thai in Wailuku is a must stop for Thai food aficionados from all islands when visiting Maui.

Traditional Hawaiian food is best found at a _lu'au_ and includes _kalua_ pork cooked in an _imu_ (underground), sweet potato, squid _lu'au_, _lomilomi_ salmon and more.

Drive-ins and chains

If all this choice sounds a little overwhelming, start with Hawai'i's version of the basic meal. Try a 'plate lunch' – the statewide institution defined by a few simple elements. You'll get a styrofoam container loaded with 'two scoop rice', plus a mound of heavily mayonnaised macaroni salad. Order one with _teriyaki_ beef, breaded pork or chicken (_katsu_), fried fish, or Spam, an unexpected passion among local people. Try Rainbox Drive In, just outside of Waikiki on Kapahulu Avenue.

DRINKS

Drinking in Hawai'i is almost as important as eating; with the blazing sun overhead, hydration is an essential part of life. Local water in the Hawaiian Islands is absolutely fine to drink; doing

so actually benefits the environment, since bottled water only creates more trash. Many restaurants and hotels have established their own in-house water filtration systems. While the local people love their soda, coconut water is now sold in restaurants and stores, and is a sweet and healthy alternative. Look for local brand Waiola – they even carry it in 7-11.

In terms of alcoholic beverages, the Mai Tai is a part of the local culture, and you'll find it on every menu. Perhaps the best place to experience a real tropical drink is an authentic tiki bar – an open-air establishment with South Pacific-style decor. Some of the best bars in the islands are actually 'barefoot bars', meaning they are situated on the sand and the management encourages patrons to take off their shoes before partaking. The best of the barefoot/tiki bars are The Hula Grill in Whaler's Village, on Maui and La Mariana Sailing Club in Honolulu (see page 109).

Beer-lovers swear by some of the local brews in Hawaii, too, namely those from the Maui Brewing Company and the Kona Brewing Company, which has restaurants in Kona on Hawai'i Island and in East Oahu as well.

In recent years a number of small-batch spirits producers have sprouted up on the islands. One of the best: Koloa Rum – available in bars and grocery and liquor stores throughout the islands. Note that in Hawai'i, like the rest of the US, the legal drinking age is 21.

Upmarket stores in Waikiki

SHOPPING

From kitschy souvenirs to luxury stores along Kalakaua Avenue, Hawai'i has it all.
Neighbor island residents travel to Oahu to shop for the basics, but they are also home
to wonderful local boutiques full of wares you can't find anywhere else in the world.

All of the Hawaiian Islands, with the exception of less-developed Molokai and Lanai, offer endless retail possibilities, from shopping centers to surf shops to small-town treasures or chic resort boutiques. Shopping is big in Hawai'i – it's not only a favorite pastime of local folks, but a big attraction for Japanese and Chinese travelers known to plan their trips around shopping holidays (such as Golden Week) and stock up at Ala Moana Center and Luxury Row. As you travel the recommended routes, you'll come across many opportunities to stop and find bits of Hawai'i to take home with you, many of which are called out in the descriptions.

SHOPPING AREAS

The malls
Ala Moana Center, the biggest outdoor mall in America, has all of the traditional big-name department stores and chains – from Abercrombie & Fitch to Neiman Marcus, and hundreds more options for the avid shopper. There are also kiosks, surf shops and restaurants. Ala Moana can be a full day of shopping, and you still might not see everything.

If you want to get all your shopping done at one time and in one place, this is the best way to do it. On Maui, the Maui Mall in Kahalui and Grand Wailea Shops at Wailea are the equivalent. On Kauai, it's Kukui Grove Center in Lihue, and on Hawai'i Island, the King's Shops Waikoloa Beach Resort.

Outdoor shop-hopping
If you prefer to take your time and enjoy Hawai'i's climate and people-watching, there are many outdoor shopping districts with eclectic mixes of treasures. The most recognized and busiest of these is Kalakaua Avenue in Waikiki, where the shopping goes on for more than a mile, starting at the west end with Luxury Row, and running all the way down to Kapiolani Park. Don't miss Waikiki Beach Walk, just off of Kalakaua Avenue on the ocean side, along Lewers Street. There's beer and sports at Yardhouse and excellent women's boutiques all in one spot here.

Pa'ia town on Maui, Ali'i Drive on the Big Island and Hanalei on Kauai all have similar atmospheres, made up of a fun mix of local specialty stores like bikini boutiques, dress shops, art galleries,

Hawaiian souvenirs   *Shops in Pa'ia*

aloha wear and cafés, along with the occasional big-box store.

Shop local

To shop like the locals and bring home clothes, jewelry and household wares like no one else has, head to the independent stores. In part because the state is so isolated, Hawai'i truly works hard to support local designers and small business owners. The Chinatown neighborhood is a must on Oahu. Start at Fighting Eel (see page 33) and don't miss Owens & Co. either. Kailua, on the windward side of Oahu, is an up-and-coming shopping area also made up of locally run small businesses. Similar mixes of local favorites can be found at Ward Village on Oahu, where Red Pineapple is the best gift shop on the island, and in Makawao on Maui.

WHAT TO BUY

While it's tempting to buy everyone back home something with the words 'aloha' or 'Hawai'i' on it, nowadays, there are excellent souvenirs you can bring home that you and everyone else will want to use. Shops like Sand People in Hanalei and Waikiki carry beachy housewares – everything from pillows to seashell light strings. Hawai'i's fashion is unique, too – bring home some Tori Richard or Ava Sky for summer parties and you'll never run into anyone wearing the same dress again.

Prices

For the best values, head out of Waikiki and the other resort towns and into the malls and local shop areas. Prices are almost always most expensive in the resort areas and there are never sales or markdowns of any sort. One exception is the T Galleria/Duty Free Shopping on Kalakaua Avenue in Waikiki, which often features local designers and does indeed have sales. Also, tax is waived – even if you're not leaving the country when done! (See page 111).

Shopping hours

Shopping hours are long in high-traffic, visitor areas like Waikiki, and generally run from 10am to 10pm. However, smaller towns and boutiques are often run by local owners and more likely to be open from 10am to 6pm. Always call ahead before driving somewhere for a specific shop, as many take a day off early in the week, too.

WHAT NOT TO BUY

As with any major tourist destination, Hawai'i has shops and vendors that sell items they should not be selling. One of the offending items is black coral, which is harvested from the waters between Maui and Lanai and is believed to be rare. It also pays to enquire about the origin of many items advertised as 'authentic' Hawaiian; upon investigation many of these items turn out to be manufactured in China or Indonesia.

Gathering of the Kings Luau

ENTERTAINMENT

Whether your idea of entertainment is enjoying a cultural show while sipping a Mai Tai or drinks at the hottest bar in town surrounded by new friends, there are opportunities to do it all on almost every Hawaiian Island.

Entertainment comes in many forms in Hawai'i – and with tourism at the heart of the state's economy, islanders want every visitor to feel entertained. Unsurprisingly, Oahu is the busiest island at night, with hip bars and sleek nightclubs. In all of the major tourist areas, you can find musicians in venues ranging from hotel bars to intimate clubs. To find the most up-to-date information, check out local newspapers and their online entertainment listings or Frolic Hawai'i (www.frolichawaii.com).

HAWAIIAN ENTERTAINMENT

For the full-scale Hawai'i cultural experience, sign on for a *lu'au*. The best pick you up, drive you to a beautiful oceanfront location and provide dinner and a show, complete with dancing, jokes and music. They can be expensive and a little bit cheesy, but it's an experience not to be missed. The best include Paradise Cove Luau on Oahu (www.paradisecove.com), Maui Nui Luau at Black Rock on Maui (www.sheraton-maui.com/dining/sunsetluau), Gathering of the Kings Luau at the Fairmont on Hawai'i Island (www.gatheringofthekings.com) and the Grand Hyatt Kauai Luau on Kauai (http://grandhyattkauailuau.com).

For a more casual experience, Hawaiian hula and music is alive and well. Hawai'i's slack key guitar, unlike anything else in the world, can be heard at nearly every hotel on Friday and Saturday evenings and there Hawaiian music concerts occur frequently at the Waikiki Shell, an outdoor amphitheater in Kapiolani Park.

SUNSET CRUISES

A number of sunset cruise companies depart from major ports on all four major islands; some, however, are better than others. These cruises, often called 'booze cruises', usually include a drink or two in the price of the tour and last around an hour. On Oahu, the **Alii Kai Catamaran** (http://aliikaicatamaran.com) is a giant ship designed to look like an ancient Polynesian vessel. On Maui, check out the **Hula Girl Dinner Cruise** (http://sailingmaui.com), a catamaran with a VIP lounge near the captain's fly bridge. On Hawai'i Island, the 'Evening on the Reef Glass Bottom Dinner Cruise', from Blue Sea Cruises (http://

First Friday in Wailuku

blueseacruisesinc.com), is designed around dolphin-spotting at sunset.

BARS AND NIGHTCLUBS

Bars in Hawai'i generally come in three flavors: swanky, dive and tiki. For the swanky spots, all of which are located in hotels, you'll need to wear long pants and sometimes even shoes, but elsewhere attire is casual; you can really pull up a barstool in your swimsuit. The best of these are in Waikiki – Sky Bar and the Library at the Modern are the best places for dancing – and, on Maui, in Wailea, Lahaina and Kaanapali. The Big Island and Kauai are more likely to have hotel and dive bars – check out Tahiti Nui (see page 105) in Hanalei and Lava Lava Beach Club at Waikoloa (see page 52). The tiki bars are worth traveling a bit to see, because you'll truly feel like you're in old Hawai'i. Head to La Mariana Sailing Club (see page 109) on Oahu for a Daddy's Rum Punch, an incredible sunset and people at the bar who might actually be pirates. It is simply the best in the state, and conveniently located near the airport.

ARTS AND DRINKS

Arts and libations come together at many evening events across the islands. These are a mix of learning more about arts and culture while socializing with the locals. Some of these include Art After Dark at the Honolulu Art Museum on the last Friday of each month (http://honolulumuseum.org/events/art_after_dark) and First Friday in Chinatown on Oahu, at Holualoa on the Big Island, and in Makawao on Maui, all of which start around sunset and run through the evening for various lengths of time.

Hula in Hawai'i

The following hula performances, sponsored by hotels and shopping centers, offer a free taste of this traditional Hawaiian dance. They don't require a long bus ride to a *lu'au*, and are located close to Waikiki hotels.

Kuhio Beach Hula Show (Tue, Thu, Sat 6.30–7.30pm), at the beachside hula mound where Uluniu Street meets Kalakaua Avenue in Waikiki.

Helumoa (Sat 6–6.30pm), at the Royal Hawaiian Center's Royal Grove's *hula kahiko* (ancient-style hula). There are also free hula lessons at Helumoa (Tue 11am, Thu 4pm). The sessions are led by Puake'ala Mann, a greatly-respected *kumu* (teacher) *hula*.

Ku Ha'aheo, to Cherish with Pride (Tue 4.30–6pm), at Waikiki Beach Walk, takes place on the Plaza Lawn on Lewers Street, in front of Yardhouse Restaurant.

Ala Moana's Hula Show (Mon–Sat 1–1.20pm), the most regularly occurring hula show, happens at the mall's center stage. The free show was created by noted *kumu hula* Kapu Dalire-Moe and is a nice complement to your shopping experience.

Zipline at Botanical World Adventures

OUTDOOR ACTIVITIES

While many visitors come to Hawai'i to sip Mai Tais in a chaise lounge near a resort pool, a growing number of other visitors fly to the islands to enjoy all of the outdoor recreation the islands have to offer. They never leave disappointed.

If you like the outdoors, there's no shortage of things to do in Hawai'i. Hiking, cycling, surfing, snorkeling, diving, swimming, stand-up paddling, kayaking, outrigger canoeing, wildlife-watching, paragliding, horseback riding, ziplining, shark-diving and deep-sea fishing are just some of the activities available. You can cycle down the flanks of a volcano, ride a motorcycle on one of the curviest roads in America, or kitesurf into the teeth of strong trade winds.

HAWAI'I BY AIR

Hawai'i has everything from sky-diving to paragliding and ziplining. On Oahu, take a seaplane tour with Island Seaplanes (http://islandseaplane.com) on Lagoon Drive, or head across the street to Novictor for a tour by helicopter (http://novictorhelicopters.com). On Kauai, check out the Na Pali Coast from the air on a flight-seeing tour with Wings Over Kauai (http://wingsover hawaii.com). Blue Hawaiian (http://blue hawaiian.com) offers trips on all four of the major islands.

Ziplining has become another big draw on the islands, with a number of facilities sprouting up. On Maui, Pi'iholo Ranch has built a spectacular zipline course. On Kauai, a number of outfitters offer the same sort of amenities; Back Country Kauai combines ziplining with inner-tubing down the open-air canals of a former sugar cane plantation (www.kauaibackcountry.com). On Oahu, Kualoa Ranch (www.kualoa.com) allows you to zipline across Kaaawa Valley, where *Jurassic Park* was filmed.

CYCLING

Hawai'i is known for cycling, in part because Kona is home to the Ironman World Championships. However, there's another great ride anyone can do: down the slopes of a volcano. This adrenaline-fueled pastime is perhaps most popular on Maui, where a number of outfitters lead early-morning trips down the slopes of Haleakala. One of the best is Bike Maui (http://bikemaui. com), whose trips include pick-up and drop-off from their store in Haiku. A word of caution: the majority of rides occur alongside automobile traffic, and cycling on any of the major roads is not recommended for children.

Sliding Sands Trail   *Learning to surf in Waikiki*

FISHING

Hawai'i is world-famous for big-game fishing, especially for catches taken off the Kona Coast of the Big Island. World-class fishing tournaments held there each summer draw competitive game fishermen from across the globe. One of the biggest is the Hawai'i International Billfish Tournament. Charter trips, on which attendants take you to their secret lucky spots and teach you their methods, include Sea Wife Charters (http://seawifecharters.com) located in Kona; several charters also depart from Lahaina and Ma'alaea on Maui, and Kewalo Basin on Oahu.

HIKING

Hawai'i is a hiker's paradise. You could hike a different trail every day for a year in Hawai'i and probably still have a few more months' worth after that. Local groups estimate the state boasts more than 3,000 miles (4,828km) of hiking trails, ranging from easy to moderate to hard. The 11-mile (18km) Kalalau Trail along the Na Pali Coast on Kauai is considered one of the best backcountry hikes in the United States, and usually requires two or three overnights to get from the trailhead near Ke'e Beach to the Kalalau Valley.

Another epic hike: the climb up Koko Head, on Oahu. It's not the length of this trail that presents a challenge for hikers (it's only 1.5 miles/2.4km long). Instead, it's the elevation gain: the trail includes more than 1,000 steps as it climbs 1,600ft (488 meters). On Maui and Hawai'i islands, just about any hike on national park land will be fulfilling. On Lanai, in places like the fire-red Garden of the Gods, you can feel as if you are on another planet.

WATER SPORTS

The islands are a great place to engage in water sports, with each place having its own specialty. Windsurfing is popular at Kailua Beach on Oahu and Ho'okipa Beach on Maui, and can be learned in a variety of windsurfing schools. Kiteboarding is similar but with a smaller board so athletes can do flips and other tricks. The Kiteboarding School of Maui (http://ksmaui.com), located in Kahului, was the first kiteboarding school in the world.

Diving is also incredibly popular in Hawai'i and is particularly good around Hawai'i Island, which has almost no soil to create runoff, leaving the water crystal clear. On Maui, a plethora of outfitters offer snorkeling trips to places such as Molokini; Pride of Maui (www.prideofmaui.com) is among the most reputable.

The Hawaiian Islands are considered to be the birthplace of modern surfing, which makes them a great place to hang ten. Amateurs usually opt for calmer spots: Waikiki Beach on Oahu, Poipu Beach on Kauai, Kahalu'u Beach Park near Kailua on Hawai'i Island, and off Lahaina on Maui. Surf schools operate in all four of these latter spots; lessons last 1–2 hours and cost anywhere from $95 to $150.

Priests row to greet Captain Cook

HISTORY: KEY DATES

From the ancient Polynesian settlers, through the arrival of the first Europeans and the Hawaiian monarchy, to the islands' designation as an American territory, Hawai'i has a rich and colorful history.

EARLY HISTORY

200–500 AD	First settlers arrive in Hawai'i, probably from the Marquesas Islands.
800–1200	Polynesian pioneers arrive, this time from Tahiti.
1750	Kamehameha (the Great) born on Hawai'i Island's northernmost point.

WESTERN INFLUENCE

1778	Captain James Cook encounters Hawaiian Islands, and names them Sandwich Islands, after his patron, the Earl of Sandwich.
1779	Cook killed in a skirmish with Hawaiians.
1790	Kamehameha I begins unification of the Hawaiian Islands by conquering Maui and Lanai.
1812	Sandalwood trade booms.
1819	Kamehameha I dies in Kailua, on Hawai'i Island. His son, Liholiho, becomes Kamehameha II, and paves way for the introduction of Christianity in the islands by abolishing the ancient *kapu* system.
1820	The first contingent of Protestant missionaries arrives in Hawai'i. The capital and royal court are moved to Lahaina, on Maui.
1825	Whaling industry begins 40-year boom.
1835	First Hawaiian sugar plantation established at Koloa, Kauai.
1845	The capital moves back to Honolulu from Lahaina.
1848	Kamehameha III enacts Great Mahele, dividing land among the crown, chiefs and commoners.
1852	The king unveils new constitution.
1869	'Big Five' company Alexander & Baldwin founded.
1872	Kamehameha V dies, ending the dynasty. He leaves no heir.
1873	Lunalilo elected king.
1874	After Lunalilo dies, Kalakaua is elected king. New monarch visits Washington, DC, to push for a reciprocity treaty with US.

Attack on the US Naval base at Pearl Harbor

1878	Thousands of immigrant plantation workers arrive, primarily from Portugal and Asia.
1887	Kalakaua signs Bayonet Constitution, which limits his power.
1889	Robert Wilcox leads unsuccessful revolt against opponents of the King.
1891	Kalakaua dies in San Francisco. His sister, Lili'uokalani, is named queen.

FALL OF THE MONARCHY

1893	Anti-royalists launch successful coup.
1894	Provisional government declares itself to be the Republic of Hawai'i.
1895	Supporters of Lili'uokalani stage a counter coup, but are defeated.
1898	President William McKinley signs legislation to annexe Hawai'i.
1900	Hawai'i becomes territory of the United States. Construction of naval base at Pearl Harbor begins.
1902	First transpacific telegraphic cable linking Hawai'i and California is laid.
1903	Prince Jonah Kuhio Kalaniana'ole begins term as Hawai'i's delegate to Congress.
1912	Hawai'i's premier surfer, Duke Kahanamoku, wins Olympic gold medal in swimming.
1917	Queen Lili'uokalani dies.
1922	James Dole's Hawaiian Pineapple Company buys island of Lanai.
1941	Japanese fighter planes bomb Pearl Harbor, propelling the United States into World War II.

STATEHOOD

1959	Hawai'i becomes 50th state.
1986	John Waihe'e, the first ethnic Hawaiian governor, takes office.
1990s	Resort development takes off along Oahu's Waikiki Beach and on Maui, Kauai and Hawai'i Island.
2002	Former Maui mayor Linda Lingle, a Republican, becomes Hawai'i's first female governor. She is re-elected in 2006.
2006	Del Monte ceases operating in Hawai'i, leaving Dole as the island's only pineapple producer.
2008	Barack Obama, a native of Hawai'i, elected US President.
2012	Larry Ellison, CEO of Oracle Corporation, buys 98 percent of the island of Lanai for a reported $600 million.
2013	State legislature legalizes same-sex marriage.

BEST ROUTES

HONOLULU SIGHTS

A perfect first day in paradise made to slowly shake off any jetlag while getting acquainted with the capital city. Did you know that there are over a million people living on O'ahu? Today you get a little taste of tropical-urban life in Honolulu.

DISTANCE: 12 miles (8km) driving, with 2 miles (3km) of walking
TIME: A half day
START: Orchids at Halekulani
END: 'Iolani Palace
POINTS TO NOTE: Ideal for a morning tour to beat the heat, this slow-paced drive and walk covers Punchbowl National Cemetery, The Honolulu Museum of Art Spalding House and Downtown Honolulu, with terrific views all along the way. You'll need to hire a car and wear walking shoes – choose a weekday to truly experience urban Honolulu, as much of it closes down on the weekend.

Waikiki's streets are busting before dawn – if jetlag has you up early, head out for a sunrise swim in the ocean – you'll be in good company. For breakfast, head to **Orchid's**, see ❶, at the **Halekulani ❶**, where the only worry you'll have is hearing your companion over the sound of the waves. Pack your walking shoes, hop in the car and follow Ala Wai Boulevard to McCully Street. The smooth brown waters of the Ala Wai Canal, built in the 1920s to empty the fishponds and marsh now called Waikiki, are on your right. Follow McCully *mauka* (towards the mountains), turn left onto South Beretania Street, then right onto Punahou Street. Before it begins climbing into Manoa Valley, turn left onto Nehoa Street, then right onto Makiki Street.

Tantalus

Round Top Drive spirals upwards through a residential area into a rainforest, breaking out at **Tantalus Lookout ❷** with vistas towards Diamond Head and Waikiki. Diamond Head crater popped up about 150,000 years ago. The ocean side is higher because the northeast trade winds deposited more ash there. Directly below you, the lush Manoa Valley opens from the Ko'olau Mountains and the University of Hawai'i campus sprawls at the valley's mouth. The road climbs further up Tantalus to **Pu'u'ualaka'a State**

View of Honolulu from Pu'u Ualaka'a State Wayside Park

Wayside Park ❸, nice for a short walk to a stupendous view, this time extending from left of Diamond Head to Ewa.

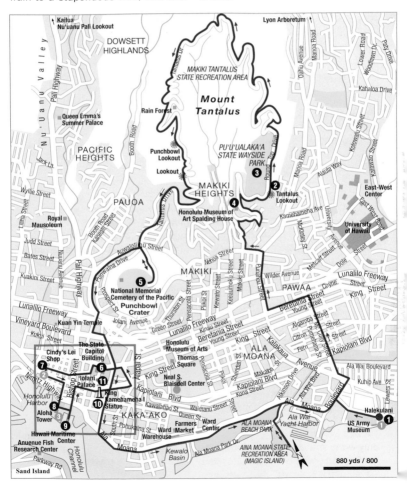

The Honolulu Museum of Art

Spalding House

Continue up Tantalus through deep and lush rainforest, circling around for miles before descending, where you'll come across the **Honolulu Museum of Art Spalding House** ❹ (https://honolulumuseum.org/11981-spalding_house; Tue–Fri 1am–4pm; free for children under 12), with artfully landscaped grounds as impressive as the art that lies inside.

Punchbowl Cemetery

After you've toured the grounds, continue down the mountain on Tantalus Road, then turn left onto Puowaina Drive, which leads you into Punchbowl Crater and the **National Memorial Cemetery of the Pacific** ❺. The Hawaiian name for Punchbowl is Puowaina, meaning hill of sacrifice. The cemetery is a somber but beautiful place.

HONOLULU WALKING TOUR

Downtown Honolulu

Puowaina Street becomes Queen Emma Street as you round the crater towards Honolulu. Park on the street or in one of many municipal lots that dot Punchbowl Street and Queen Emma. The **State Capitol Building** ❻, with its pillars representing palm trees around the open-centered, volcano-shaped building, is located on the corner of Punchbowl and Beretania streets. On the Beretania side is a statue of Father Damien, priest to the Molokai leper

colony. It faces Washington Place, built in 1846 by Queen Lili'uokalani's husband's family, and is now home to Hawai'i's Governor. After walking through the capital to experience the art and architecture, walk down Richards Street along the west side of the building, then right onto Hotel Street. Although urban renewal has gentrified portions of Hotel Street, some parts remain a rowdy strip, a contemporary offshoot of the days when sailors on shore leave swarmed its sidewalks.

Chinatown

Proceeding down Hotel Street you'll reach Chinatown. Head right on Bethel Street for local fashion and boutiques, and to view the beautifully restored Hawai'i Theatre, built in 1927. Check with the box office for upcoming per-

State Capitol Building

Dim sum in Chinatown   *Chinatown market*

formances, then consider shopping at any of the local boutiques along Bethel – Fighting Eel, created by two local designers, is especially popular with local fashionistas.

Chinatown is thick with old buildings and culture. Head left onto Pauahi Street, then left at Maunakea Street, where you'll find the island's best *lei* shops. Flowers of every type are woven, strung and tied into beautiful variations of *lei* that line the refrigerators in the small open shops of Maunakea Street. Stop in and poke

around, smell the *lei* and ask questions – the friendly proprietors are full of knowledge. **Cindy's Lei Shop** ❼ (www.cindys leishoppe.com; daily 6am–6pm) has a particularly wide range.

Continue down Maunakea Street, then left on King Street, all the while poking through vegetable stalls, acupuncture clinics, herbalists, noodle factories, antique stores and eateries. **The Pig and the Lady**, see ❷, is on your right – you've just found Honolulu's hottest, trendiest lunch and din-

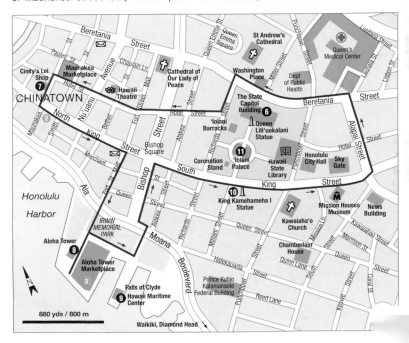

Magic Island

Across from Ala Moana Shopping Center, the largest outdoor mall in America, sits Ala Moana Park and Magic Island, officially known as Aina Moana State Recreation Area. Magic Island is a wonderful place for a walk or run, to watch the sunset, or simply to sit and watch a cultural theater of people at play. You can watch surfers close up at Ala Moana Bowls, and the view back towards Diamond Head and Waikiki is the one you see in postcards.

Magic Island serves as an important local gathering place. Not only do local fairs, walks, runs and fundraisers all occur in the park, but it's also a place where extended families and friends spend weekends and holidays, popping up tents for shade, setting up tables and staying all day and well into the night in their beach chairs. It's the go-to spot for a potluck, a baby's first birthday *lu'au* and other local traditions. The enclosed, dredged lagoon is a comfortable place to swim for those not well-acquainted with ocean swimming, there's plenty of parking, and there's always an event of some sort going on – from lawn-bowling to a cultural festival.

Pick up some take-out, catch the sunset on a Friday evening, then turn around and face Diamond Head for the weekly fireworks show at the Hilton Hawaiian Village for a perfect evening. You might even get invited in to one of the parties.

ner spot. Not for the faint of heart or vegetarian – if you're really hungry you can order the entire pig's head.

Aloha Tower and maritime history

When you've had your fill, follow Fort Street Mall to the waterfront. Since 1926, **Aloha Tower** ❽ (daily 9.30am–5pm; free) has been greeting tourists arriving by boat. Take the elevator to the top to catch the view of the harbor and city below from 10 stories up.

From the tower, it's two minutes to the Falls of Clyde, built in 1878 and used as a passenger ship between Honolulu and San Francisco. Visit the **Hawai'i Maritime Center** ❾ right by it, which has eclectic displays from surfboards to ancient canoes, and peek into the long history of whaling in the Pacific.

King Kamehameha Statue

'Iolani Palace

If you weren't tempted by the Pig and the Lady, **Gordon Biersch**, see ❸, one of a chain of brewery restaurants across America, has a prime waterfront location and open-air bar at the end of Aloha Tower Marketplace. With plenty of seats, great beer and garlic fries, it's the perfect stop to rest weary feet and refuel while enjoying the view of Honolulu Harbor.

'Iolani Palace and King Kamehameha
Bishop Street leads back downtown, dominated by banks and corporate loftiness. Turn right on King Street to the **King Kamehameha I statue** ❿. This is a duplicate; the original statue,

lost at sea then later recovered, now stands on the Big Island. Opposite the monument is **'Iolani Palace** ⓫ (www.iolanipalace.org; free for children under 4 during guided tours: every 10 minutes Mon 9am–4pm, Tue–Thu 10.30am–4pm, Fri–Sat noon–4pm; no reservation required), completed in 1882 by King Kalakaua. From 1893 until 1969, after the monarchy's fall, the palace was the capitol for the republic, territory and finally the state. The palace is open for tours Monday through Saturday. The self-paced audio tour allows you to enjoy as much or as little of the palace as you'd like.

Food and Drink

❶ ORCHIDS AT THE HALEKULANI

2199 Kalia Road; tel: 844-288 8402; www.halekulani.com/dining/orchids-restaurant; daily 7.30–11am, 11.30am–2pm and 6–10pm; $$$$
This place screams casual elegance, if elegance screamed, that is. One of the top restaurants in the state, it's famous for Sunday brunch, but great for everything else, too, including a light breakfast while the sun comes up over Diamond Head.

❷ THE PIG AND THE LADY

83 N. King Street; tel: 808-585 8255; www.thepigandthelady.com; daily 10.30am–2pm and 5.30–10.30pm; $$

The Pig and the Lady started as a food truck with lines around the block. Now they have a hip, exposed-brick restaurant with picnic table family-style dining and unique cocktails. Reservations available. If you have a big party, try the entire pig's head – strange, but surprisingly delicious.

❸ GORDON BIERSCH

1 Aloha Tower Drive 1123; tel: 808-599 4877; www.gordonbiersch.com/locations/honolulu; Sun–Thu 11am–11pm, Fri 11–12.30am, Sat 11am–midnight; $$
Part brewery, part restaurant, part boat-watching – and always relaxed. Indoor and outdoor dining with a perfect burger and fries. Try the beer sampler before you commit to your beer.

View from Nu'uanu Pali Lookout

CIRCLE O'AHU AND NORTH SHORE

This tour encircles the Ko'olau Mountain Range, leading out of Honolulu, past the green, steep cliffs of windward O'ahu, to the Mecca of big wave surfing. Experience country-living, sacrificial heiaus and empty beaches.

DISTANCE: 95 miles (154km) roundtrip
TIME: A full day
START: Pali Highway
END: Bishop Museum
POINTS TO NOTE: This is an all-day adventure, so plan to hit the road early. There are three routes from Honolulu through the Ko'olau Mountains to the windward side: H-3 through Halawa, Likelike Highway or the Pali Highway. Take the latter for the best views. Pack swimsuits, towels, snorkels and masks (in summer). Car activities for kids are a good idea as there are some long stretches in the car.

WINDWARD O'AHU

Even the *kama'aina* take this tour from time to time – it serves as a mini-break from reality and reminder of the paradise they live in. From Honolulu, take the **Pali Highway** ❶ north, or *mauka* (towards the mountains) from downtown Honolulu. The highway climbs steadily up Nu'uanu Valley. Just before the top and

the first of two short tunnels, pull off for **Nu'uanu Pali State Park** ❷, also known as the Pali Lookout, and open from dawn to dusk, for stunning views of the coast you'll soon travel. Among the strange local lore is the standing rule that you must never take pork over the Pali. The reason is unknown, but many locals refrain from doing so nonetheless.

The Koolau Range is the remnant of O'ahu's younger volcano, and the windward side's steep, often waterfall-lined cliffs rise up to 3,000ft (915 meters). Kane'ohe is left, and Kailua is right. The spire across the way is the 1,643ft (501 meters) Olomana, home to a popular but treacherous hike complete with ropes to climb to the top – only for the very experienced. Continue over the Pali, turning left onto Kamehameha Highway (Route 83) at the first signal after the tunnels. Don't go straight, which leads to Kailua or southeast O'ahu (see page 42).

On Kamehameha Highway, look left if it's rainy above the cliffs, as it usually is, and you might be fortunate enough to catch waterfalls pouring down the

Byodo-In Temple   *Jungle Tour at Kualoa Ranch*

cliffs. The highway jogs left in Kaneohe town – be careful to go left at the big intersection (follow the signs to Likelike Highway), then turn right again shortly thereafter onto Kahekili Highway (still Route 83, curiously enough). Follow signs to Kahaluu and the North Shore.

Valley of the Temple
Just through Kaneohe you'll come across a valley of cemeteries. This is Valley of the Temples. Turn left onto Avenue of the Temple and follow the road up, up, up to **Byodo-In** ❸ (www.byodo-in.com), a stunning replica of a Japanese temple. Built in 1968 to commemorate the centennial of Hawai'i's first Japanese immigrants, you'll feel you've left Hawai'i and landed in Japan.

Jurassic valley
Return to the highway and continue on, hugging the shoreline through primal-looking terrain and ironwood-lined coastlines. **Kualoa Ranch** ❹ (www.kualoa.com; tour reservations recommended), where *Jurassic Park*, *Lost* and many other movies and TV programs were filmed, is on the left, just opposite Chinaman's Hat, properly called Mokoli'i. The ranch offers horseback and ATV tours for movie-lovers, but consider going even if not a movie buff, as the tour of Kaaawa Valley is stunning.

Canned culture
By now, you've probably seen the ubiquitous advertisements in Waikiki for

The Polynesian Cultural Center ❺, which is owned and operated by the Mormon Church. Clearly, many visitors enjoy the park, which provides a Disneyland approach to Pacific Island cultures. The staffers are all islanders (students from neighboring Brigham Young University's Hawai'i campus), full of contagious good spirits, and well versed in the cultures they represent. It's not like going to Tahiti or Samoa, and the playful interactive chatter with visitors may be a bit predictable, but it can none the less be fun and is certainly informative.

NORTH SHORE

A few miles further on and you'll reach Kahuku, a quiet former sugar plantation town that now serves as a center of Hawaiian aquaculture. You've arrived on the North Shore, the surfing capital of the world. Make a lunch stop at **Funi's Shrimp**, see ❶, the best of the roadside trucks that serves fresh prawns – your lunch was likely swimming yesterday. Expect to have the biggest and best prawns you've ever tasted.

Turtle Bay Resort
Turtle Bay Resort ❻ (www.turtlebayresort.com), the north shore's only resort, is up next. Their tagline, Hawai'i's Fabled North Shore, rings true here – you are now in the thick of Surfin', U.S.A. At the **Hang Ten Bar and Grill**, see ❷, pool bar, surfers pass by 20ft (6 meters) offshore while you enjoy a tropi-

Turtle Bay Resort

cal drink – the Skinny Coco is highly recommended. The hotel offers the perfect alternative to Waikiki for those looking to experience the rural north shore in lieu of an urban hotel.

Famous beaches

Partway along the 2-mile (3km) -long **Sunset Beach** ❼ is a long stretch of parking directly on the highway – look for the lifeguard stand. In summer, it's

Surfers at Banzai Pipeline

a lovely place to swim and beachcomb. Look for large cone shells and even the rare and coveted sunrise shell in the shallow water just beyond the shore break. Across from Sunset Elementary School, turn into Ehukai Beach Park to find the infamous **Banzai Pipeline ⑧**. If it's summertime, you'll wonder what the fuss is all about, as there's probably hardly a ripple, much less a wave, in sight. Come back in winter when waves reach 30ft (9 meters) and upwards for the real experience. If you're there during a swell, the steep beach sets up a natural amphitheater, making it easy to watch the incredible show of surfing just 20yds/meters offshore.

Historical sites

Just before Waimea Bay, turn left at the Foodland grocery store, climbing the road to the **Pu'uomahuka Heiau ⑨**, on your right at the top of the hill. This is the largest _iau_, a large open-air temple 300ft (100 meters) above the sea, on O'ahu. One can only hope that the view mellowed the misery of sacrificial victims in 1792, among them some hapless British sailors. Behind Waimea Bay and the beach, a road leads to **Waimea Valley ⑩** (www.waimeavalley. net), an archeologically important site surrounded by 1,800 acres (728 hectares) of nature preserve accessed by mountain bike, all terrain vehicle or on foot. The park switches ownership regularly, and with that opening hours and things like the availability of tours (as opposed to self-guided hikes) changes too, so check the website before planning your trip.

The biggest waves ever ridden are foud at **Waimea Bay ⑪**. In summer you

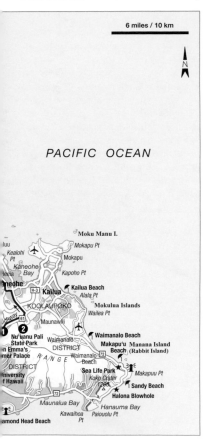

6 miles / 10 km

PACIFIC OCEAN

Moku Manu I.

luu
Kealohi Pt
Mokapu Pt
Mokapu
Kaneohe Bay
Kapoho Pt
ieeia
neohe
H-3 Kailua
Kailua Beach
Alala Pt
KO'OLAUPOKO
Mokulua Islands
Wailea Pt
Maunawili

Nu'uanu Pali State Park
n Emma's
mer Palace
Waimanalo
DISTRICT
Waimanalo Beach
Makapu'u Beach
Manana Island (Rabbit Island)
R A N G E
Waimanalo Beach
DISTRICT
University f Hawaii
Sea Life Park
Koko Crater
1260
Makapuu Pt
72
Sandy Beach
Halona Blowhole
Maunalua Bay
Hanauma Bay
Kawaihoa Pt
Paiouolu Pt
amond Head Beach

Cliff-diving at Waimea Bay

can wait your turn in line with the locals to leap off the rock,. Expect fun, light-hearted pier pressure if you climb up! The water is clearer in summer than any swimming pool you've ever seen, and spinner dolphins are often in the bay in the morning. They love the company of snorkelers.

Haleiwa

Next, head for **Hale'iwa** ⑫, the North Shore's center for local shopping and dining. On weekends, heavy traffic makes a North Shore drive slow, but there are plenty of places to stop en route. For fish and ocean views, head for **Haleiwa Joe's**, see ③, or stop for coffee and pastries at the **Coffee Gallery**, see ④, tucked away in the North Shore Marketplace, south of town. The seven-layer bar is just the kick you need for the long drive back to town.

Either head back toward Honolulu on Route 99, or continue along the coast to Mokuleia for miles of beaches you'll have all to yourself. If you continue on, go to the end of the road for the hour-long walk to **Ka'ena Point** ⑬, O'ahu's western tip. It's believed that the spirits of the dead come here to depart earth, however, you're more likely to encounter endangered Hawaiian Monk Seals (look close – when napping they look like large rocks!) or nesting albatross here in winter.

PINEAPPLE HILLS

From Hale'iwa, take Route 99 south through fields of sugar and pineapple.

There are no bargains, or even free samples, at the touristy **Dole Pineapple Pavilion** ⑭ (www.dole-plantation. com) but the adjacent topiary maze, the largest in the world, is a fun diversion for children or adults looking to stretch their legs.

Follow the intersection's left fork a bit to a signal: left leads to Whitmore Village and right empties into a field of pineapple plants, where you'll find the **Kukaniloko Birth Stones** ⑮, marked with petroglyphs and once used by *ali'i* for giving birth. Take all valuables with you from your car. Interstate H-2 empties you onto Interstate H-1 – towards Honolulu. Consider stopping at the **USS Arizona Memorial Visitor Center** ⑯ (see page 47) here, but only if you've been quick. The memorial takes time and includes a boat ride – reservations are necessary.

Exit H-1 at the Likelike Highway to find **Bishop Museum** ⑰ (www.bishop museum.org; daily 9am–5pm), the Pacific equivalent of the Smithsonian. Take a right on School Street, then another right on Kapalama Street and follow the signs. Highly recommended for those seeking to experience the rich history and culture of Hawai'i. Like the Smithsonian, hours can be spent exploring the Bishop Museum. It is a trip unto itself rather than a squeeze into another itinerary.

The museum was founded in 1889 by Charles Reed Bishop as a memorial to his wife, the last direct descendant

USS Arizona Memorial   *The Bishop Museum*

of the Kamehameha dynasty, Princess Bernice Pauahi. Her collection of heirlooms were the museum's first holdings, but in the 125-plus years since, the collection has expanded to comprise Oceania's finest specimens, both natural and human-made. Its collection is comprehensive and even overwhelming: some 200,000 artifacts; 6,000,000 shells; 250,000 plant specimens; and 13,500,000 insects.

The museum coordinates extensive archeological and sociological research throughout the Pacific. Only a small portion of its collection is on display, but the displays are formidable, especially in the cavernous and restored koa-paneled Hawaiian Hall that houses carved and feathered icons, capes and other remnants of pre-contact Hawai'i. You'll find craft demonstrations, an active volcano replica, a planetarium and Hawaiian food from local favorite Highway Inn.

Food and Drink

❶ FUMI'S SHRIMP
56-777 Kamehameha Highway (official address); tel: 808-232 8881; daily 10am–7.30pm; $
For the freshest shrimp you'll ever experience, pull over at the trucks located just past Kahuku town at Fumi's Shrimp. The menu is simple: shrimp. Try them all. The official address is 56-777 Kamehameha Highway, but don't expect a mailbox. And it's unlikely anyone will answer the telephone – they're too busy serving shrimp!

❷ HANG TEN BAR AND GRILL
Turtle Bay Resort, 57-091 Kamehameha Highway; tel: 808-293 6000; www.turtlebay resort.com; Mon–Fri 11am–8pm, open later at weekends, but unofficially; $$
Hit the Hang Ten Bar and Grill poolside. The Skinny Coco is simply perfect, and the burger and fries are great for watching the surfers fly by.

❸ HALEIWA JOE'S
66-011 Kamehameha Highway; tel: 808-637 8000; www.haleiwajoes.com; Sun–Thu 11.30am–3.30pm and 5–9.30pm, Fri–Sat 11.30am–3.30pm and 5–10.30pm; $$–$$$
Overlooking Haleiwa Harbor, just past the arched bridge, sits Haleiwa Joe's. This is where the locals come for a fancy fish dinner. North Shore fancy means shorts and slippers are ok, but consider an *aloha* shirt if you have one. Sit outside to enjoy the view, and be sure to order the fresh fish.

❹ THE COFFEE GALLERY
66-250 Kamehameha Highway; tel: 808-637 5355; www.roastmaster.com; daily 6.30am–8pm; $
Located in the North Shore Marketplace, the Coffee Gallery has been a Haleiwa landmark since 1987. The Hawaiian Paradise blend is hand-roasted and the baked treats are divine.

Hanauma Bay

SOUTHEAST O'AHU LOOP

A short, beach-lover's trip that's a taste of local life in the suburban neighborhoods, with a dash of world-class snorkeling, beaches and magical ocean views. This route takes you to the best beach in the world, past Sea Life Park, to a favorite local shave ice spot, before looping back to Waikiki.

DISTANCE: 35 miles (56km) roundtrip
TIME: A half day
START: Kapiolani Park
END: Pali Highway, Honolulu
POINTS TO NOTE: This itinerary is ideal for families – adventures without long hours in a car. A short, paved 'hike' leads up to a lookout and is great for active people of all ages – pack the stroller for little ones, and bring your snorkeling gear, swimsuit and towel. Note: Don't start this excursion in late afternoon, as rush hour traffic goes in the same direction.

EAST O'AHU

East O'ahu, Honolulu's affluent suburban area is also home to some of its most pristine beaches. Even the locals love Waimanalo and a climb up to Makapu'u Lighthouse to whale watch. From **Kapi'olani Park ❶** in Waikiki follow Kalakaua Avenue to Diamond Head Road, continuing around Diamond Head, where the road becomes Kahala Avenue, past oceanfront mansions to Hunakai Street. Turn right onto Kilauea Avenue, past Kahala Mall, and turn right onto Waialae Ave, beneath the H-1, which turns into Kalanianaole Highway east here. After several sleepy neighborhoods, the road climbs up and to the left.

Hanauma Bay, Blowhole and Sandy Beach

At the crest on the right is the road to **Hanauma Bay ❷** (Wed–Mon dawn to dusk; free for children under 12). As many as 10,000 people visit the bay daily. The snorkeling is still the best on the island if you don't mind the crowds. The information center and required video prior to entry are educational and fun. Go early to beat the tour buses.

O'ahu

The coast beyond Hanauma Bay is rugged, sculpted, and dramatic – testimony to the ocean's powerful erosive effect on the islands. **Halona Blow-**

Makapu'u Lighthouse

Shoreline near Halona Blowhole

hole ❸ – where water is forced up geyser-like through a hole in the basalt – is a popular stop. The blowhole is best viewed from above, as many tourists, and locals too, are swept from the cliffs each year when they venture for a closer look. Just beyond, the road flattens out. The big beach is **Sandy Beach** ❹, one of O'ahu's most popular beaches. However, the unique conditions that make it a superb bodysurfing place also make it very dangerous. Before going in the water, check with the lifeguards. Swimming is not recommended.

To the lighthouse

The next stop is at the top of the **Makapu'u Lookout** ❺. It's easy to zip right past the overlook when cresting the top, but it's worth stopping for the view up O'ahu's windward coast, which is one of Hawai'i's best. **Makapu'u Lighthouse** ❻ stands tall on the top of the point. The 1-mile (1.6km) climb up Lighthouse Road boasts panoramic views of mountains and sea, islands and beaches, and maybe even whale and turtle sightings. There are no restrooms or services, and often not that many people. It's fairly gentle terrain, so any shoes will do.

Sea Life Park

Across from Makapu'u is **Sea Life Park** ❼, whose attractions include the world's only wolphin (half whale, half dolphin), porpoise shows, hammerhead sharks, touch pools for children, and a 300,000-gallon (1.1-million-liter) simulated reef tank. There are penguins too!

Three miles (5km) north is the town of Waimanalo, a touch of rural Hawai'i on an increasingly urban island. As you enter Waimanalo, you might recognize a house on the ocean side – Magnum P.I.'s place (well, Robin's really). Park at **Kaiona Beach Park** ❽ and walk back along the coast to see the house

Waimanolo Beach

and ocean pool. You're now at the east end of **Waimanalo Beach** ⑨, recently named the best in the world by American beach expert Dr. Beach (www.drbeach.org). It is one of the longest and nicest white sand beaches anywhere. It's nearly empty on weekdays, but break-ins are frequent, so lock the car and don't leave valuables visible.

Waimanalo to Kailua

Depending on the season, you'll see vendors selling everything from fresh fish to corn, mangoes and papayas along the highway. Look for the red and white building on your right as you come into town – **Keneke's**, see ①, is the spot for plate lunch and shave ice. Try the local favorite chicken katsu plate, and rainbow shave ice for dessert.

Continue past the needle-like peak of Olomana, the remnants of a vol-

canic dike from the old Koolau caldera located here over two million years ago. On the left is the intersection with Route 61, Pali Highway, and the way back to Honolulu and Waikiki. Right leads to the beach town **Kailua** ⑩, a haven for windsurfers and kite boarders, and where President Obama spends holiday vacations with his family. Just before it starts climbing to Nu'uanu Pali, a junction to Route 83 connects you with Route 2 (see page 36), continuing north along the coast.

Wind surfer at Kailua Beach Park

Food and Drink

① KENEKE'S

41-857 Kalanianaole Highway; tel: 808-259 9800; www.kenekes.net; daily 9am–8pm; $
This is where the locals and tourists alike go for plate lunch – Hawai'i's lunch of choice that includes a meat, rice and macaroni salad. The katsu, while not the best for you, is worth the splurge. Wash it all down with local delight shave ice – it's meant to be eaten while soaking up the sun.

Entertainment at Makahiki restaurant

WEST O'AHU

Take the road less traveled, by tourists at least, to find West O'ahu's prettiest, emptiest beaches and a touch of Disney in Hawai'i, and to experience Hawai'i's important role in World War II.

DISTANCE: 80 miles (129km)
TIME: A full day
START: Waikiki
END: USS *Arizona* Memorial
POINTS TO NOTE: This route is great for beach-lovers of all ages, and includes a stop for Disney fans who want to see Mickey in Hawai'i. If you're more interested in history than beaches, head straight to the USS *Arizona*, then tack on the Bishop Museum (see page 40). You'll be traveling against the flow of traffic, but try to avoid returning around 5pm on a workday as there can be queues coming back into Honolulu.

West O'ahu is truly a place of local people, with limited resorts – only Ko Olina has thrived where others have failed – it's untouched and authentic. The beaches go for miles, the homes are humble and the people are straightforward and kind. West side residents have a reputation for being tougher on tourists, but you'll find that anyone you greet with respect in Hawai'i will be welcoming and helpful.

Disney breakfast at Aulani

From Waikiki, drive to the H1 and go west. On a weekday, you may encounter traffic for the first couple of miles on the highway, but it will end just past downtown. H1 takes a jaunt over to the airport – stay to the left (on H201) and do not take the airport/H-1 exit. H201 reconnects with H1 later and is the faster route.

Stick to H1 all the way to the end, where you see the resorts of **Ko Olina** ❶. Exit for Ko Olina, and follow the road in past the guard shack to the **Aulani Resort** ❷, on your right. At **Makahiki** restaurant, see ❶, breakfast includes visits from Disney characters that will delight Disney fans of all ages. After the meal, tour the grounds, but don't try to swim – the resort is notoriously stingy with its pool – even friends of guests are not allowed to swim here.

Yokohama Bay

Leave the resort area, and continue west as H1 turns into Farrington Highway. Travel through the small west-side towns of Nakakuli, Waianae and Makaha, until the road ends at **Yokohama Bay** ❸. Park your car here, and if you're up for a hike,

Ka'ena Point, looking toward Yokohama Bay

you can reach **Ka'ena Point** ❹, some 2.5 miles (4km) out along a dirt coastal road (see page 40). A snorkel here is recommended. The shore break is strong, but usually quite small, and it's best to swim in front of the lifeguard stand. Dive close to the sand – this beach is full of hidden treasures in the form of cone, miter and even sometimes sunrise shells.

Makaha Beach

After your swim at Yokohama, head back along the coast to **Makaha Beach** ❺, a famous surf spot known around the world. Look for a lifeguard stand on the ocean side, just past the high-rise condominium Mahaka Shores. This is a great swimming hole and beachcombing location.

Electric Beach

Snorkeling enthusiasts will find yet another swim stop across from the power plant just past Nanakuli. Signs read **Kahe Point Beach Park** ❻ (www.livingoceans cuba.com), but locals call it Electric Beach. If you've had enough for one day, but want to see this incredible reef, consider the boat snorkeling and lunch tour. They usually get a visit from the spinner dolphins, too.

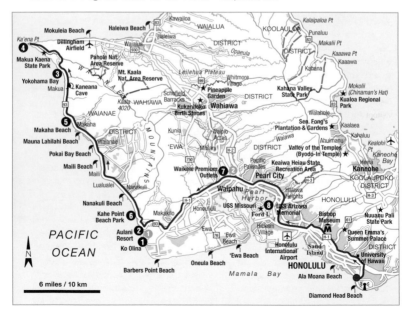

Onboard the USS Bowfin

Battleship USS Missouri

Waikele outlets

The **Waikele Premium Outlets ❼**, just off the highway to the mountain side from the Waikele exit, have more than 50 outlet stores, including Coach, Off 5th and Barneys New York. Look out for the **Leonard's Bakery** *malasada* truck, see ❷.

USS Arizona Memorial

The **USS *Arizona* Memorial ❽** (www.nps. gov) is Hawai'i's biggest attraction – and a somber, educational experience for all. Buy your tickets in advance to avoid long waits. Expect lots of sun a quick boat ride in Pearl Harbor, and remember to leave your purse and bags in the car, as they will not be allowed in for security reasons. If time allows, check out the USS *Bowfin* Submarine Museum and Park (see box).

Food and Drink

❶ MAKAHIKI

92-1185 Ali'inui Drive, Kapolei; tel: 808-674 6330; https://resorts.disney.go.com/aulani-hawaii-resort/dining; daily 7–11am and 5–9pm; $$$–$$$$

Aulani's Makahiki is pricey, but all about the Disney experience. Recommended for breakfast, when characters meet and greet visitors. Food is a very family-friendly buffet. Reservations highly recommended, validated valet parking.

❷ LEONARD'S BAKERY

933 Kapahulu Avenue, Honolulu; tel: 808-737 5591; www.leonardshawaii.com; Sun–Thu 5.30am–10pm, Fri–5.30am–11pm; $

Leonard's has a traveling truck dishing up delicious *malasadas* that is almost always located at Waikele Premium Outlets next to Old Navy. If you miss it there, taste these deep-fried, sugar-coated Portuguese doughnuts at Leonard's Bakery in Waikiki.

World War II in Hawai'i

In December 7, 1941, the Japanese attack on Pearl Harbor changed everything in Hawai'i. The military presence grew greatly as the then territory became the hub for America in the war. Over 1,000 sailors died on the USS *Arizona* that day, when a series of Japanese torpedoes and aerial bombs sank the battleship in less than 10 minutes. The remains of many are still entombed in the hull visible from the memorial, a somber reminder of the great loss.

Next door to the *Arizona* visitor center is the privately-owned USS *Bowfin* Submarine Museum and Park (www.bowfin.org), home to a World War II submarine credited with sinking 44 ships. The museum traces submarine history from 1914 to the nuclear submarine age. A shuttle links the USS *Bowfin* Museum to the Battleship *Missouri*, docked off Ford Island. It was aboard the *Missouri*, on September 2, 1945, that General Douglas MacArthur officially accepted the surrender of the Japanese military and signed the armistice that ended World War II.

Duke Kahanamoku Statue

WAIKIKI WALK

Waikiki may be a place to love and hate at the same time, but somehow it all works – the hotels, condominiums, shops, restaurants and beach. What's more, it's got the best people-watching anywhere, with resplendent sunsets to boot. Explore on foot to find hidden neighborhoods and sights, including an urban giraffe in the tropics.

DISTANCE: 6 miles (10km) roundtrip walk
TIME: 2–3 hours
START: Duke Kahanamoku Statue
END: International Market Place
POINTS TO NOTE: Start early (before 9am if you plan to hike) or late (after 3pm, if you're not intending to hike to the crater rim) to avoid the highest heat of the day.

Waikiki has a long history, and is so much more than simply a cluster of hotels. Work your souvenir shopping into this ramble around the heart of Hawai'i's tourism industry.

Duke Kahanamoku

Start at the famed **Duke Kahanamoku Statue ❶** located along Kalakaua on Waikiki Beach at Uluniu Street. Behind the statue, surfers crowd the easy-learning waves of Canoes and Baby Queens, the perfect place for surf lessons, available from any of the beach stands.

Head east, and five minutes by foot towards Diamond Head is the 200-plus-acre (81-hectare) **Kapi'olani Park ❷**,

embracing a zoo, aquarium, weekend art festivals, an outdoor concert venue (Waikiki Shell) and plenty of open space for playing. The **Waikiki Aquarium ❸** (www.waikikiaquarium.org; daily 9am–4.30pm) is a short visit and home to endangered species, such as the Hawaiian Monk Seal.

Past the aquarium see the **Natatorium War Memorial ❹**, where Kahanamoku swam when training for Olympic gold. The pool is now closed, but still worth a look, as the building is a beautiful tribute.

Diamond Head

You'll join the droves of runners and walkers that continue past the end of the park and up to **Diamond Head Lookout ❺** to watch surfers year-round and whales in the winter. Continue up and around the crater, hugging Diamond Head Road, to the entrance to **Diamond Head Crater ❻** on the left. For the ambitious, the hike up to the peak takes less than an hour and involves many stairs to the 761ft (232-meter) summit.

Continue along the road, which becomes Monsarrat Avenue, for beautiful views of Waikiki and into a sweet neigh-

Waikiki Aquarium   *Waikiki from the summit of Diamond Head*

borhood market area. The acai bowls at **Bogart's Café**, see 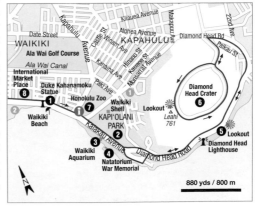❶, are famous with locals, and while open all day, breakfast here is the perfect reward for the hill you just climbed. The top bikini selection on island can be found at the quaint blue cottage called Beach House on your right.

Turn right onto Paki Avenue and catch a glimpse of the giraffes at the **Honolulu Zoo** ❼ (www.honoluluzoo.com; daily 9am–4.30pm), on your left. The zoo is ideal for kids, though always very, very hot.

Shopping Waikiki

Turn left onto Kanekapolei and back down to Kalakaua for some of the shopping that brings even the locals into Waikiki: Urban Outfitters in the Hyatt, Hawai'i's oldest and most authentic *aloha* attire company, Tori Richard in the Moana Surfrider, local designers Fighting Eel in the Royal Hawaiian Center and a plethora of modern shops at the rebuilt, once iconic, **International Market Place** ❽, no longer full of kiosks and bars, but still home to a banyan tree thought to be more than 100 years old. Once the site of Queen Emma's getaway, the center is filled with historical tidbits – Don Ho got his start here and Duke Kahanamoku himself owned a bar here, too. Finish your walk at **Mai Tai Bar**, see ❷, where the view is like a postcard.

Food and Drink

❶ BOGART'S CAFÉ

3045 Monsarrat Avenue; tel: 808-739 0999; www.bogartscafe.webs.com; Mon–Fri 6am–6.30pm, Sat–Sun 6am–6pm; $

Nestled at the foot of Diamond Head, this is a place where locals come together and smart visitors join them. The bagels with lox, smoothies and acai are all recommended.

❷ MAI TAI BAR

Royal Hawaiian Hotel, 2259 Kalakaua Avenue; tel: 808-923 7311; www.royal-hawaiian.com/dining/maitaibar; daily 10am–11.30pm; $$–$$$

A truly casual beachside bar with a healthy dose of people-watching and live music at sunset. The bar backs up its name – its Mai Tai is the best.

KOHALA AND NORTH KONA

This drive takes you through rugged lava fields and up into the mountains, to art both ancient and contemporary, beautiful cliff-side towns, Hawai'i's biggest ranch and historical sites such as Kamehameha's birthplace. There are local eats and drinks along the way, after you've worked up an appetite with a downstream kayak adventure.

DISTANCE: 150 miles (241km) roundtrip
TIME: A full day
START: Kona Airport
END: Ali'i Drive
POINTS TO NOTE: This driving tour includes quite a bit of time in the car. Start early as you'll need the full day to see everything. Pack a pair of sneakers for walking around and a swimsuit and towel – the beaches along the way will certainly tempt you!

THE KOHALA COAST

The Queen Kaahumanu Highway traverses miles of black, barren lava flows, most recently from 1859. Just north of **Kona Airport ❶**, the exclusive, very upscale **Kukio ❷** and **Four Seasons Hualalai ❸** nestle on the beach. Beach access to pristine Kukio beach is possible; pull into Kukio Road and ask at the guardhouse. The beach is pristine and usually empty, fronted by the private homes and facilities of luxurious Kukio.

Stick to the sand and water, and you'll be welcome here.

Kawaihae

Back on the highway, North Kona becomes South Kohala with a string of resorts – pass on by for now. At the junction leading to North Kohala's west coast, stop at the **Pu'ukohola Heiau ❹**, a national historic site. Dedicated to the war god, it was built by King Kamehameha I in 1791. Follow Route 270 past Kawaihae, a commercial port and the site where Kamehameha's canoes set off for conquest. **Lapakahi State Historical Park ❺** is a look back into the past of 600 years ago; in the early morning coolness it's a satisfying self-guided walk through this ghost town of a commoners' fishing village.

The road ascends inland over increasingly green hills as you climb towards Hawi. Take the **Upolu Point ❻** turnoff, where a modest straight-arrow road leads (after a left at the airstrip) to a passable (except when wet) dirt road to the **Mo'okini Heiau ❼**, a temple maintained by the same family for 1,000 years. Nearby is Kamehameha's Birthplace, *c.*1752.

Black sand beach in Pololu Valley

Hawi and Kapa'au

The main road takes you through Hawi, a one-time sugar boom-town, and turn-around for the world-renowned Ironman World Championship. In Hawi, sign up for the Flumin' Kohala Ditch (www.adventure inhawaii.com), an exhilarating kayak through otherwise inaccessible wilderness of the Kohala Mountains. From Hawi head to Kapa'au, where the original **King Kamehameha Statue ❽** stands before the unassuming Civic Center. At the road's end is the **Pololu Valley Lookout ❾**, teasing visitors with peeks of sheer ocean cliffs and a black sand beach below. From Kapa'au, turn south onto Route 250, which climbs the Kohala

mountains with spectacular views of Mauna Kea (13,677ft/4,168 meters) and Mauna Loa (13,679ft/4,169 meters) then descends into Waimea.

WAIMEA

Rustic ranching town

Waimea retains its ranch town feel despite recent gentrification. Parker Ranch, the largest individually-held ranch in America, is the dominant economic force. Don't be confused by Waimea's several names – only the post office calls the town Kamuela. In town, **Merriman's**, see ❶, is an island classic for a sit-down meal. Also notable, and more casual, is **Pau**, see ❷,

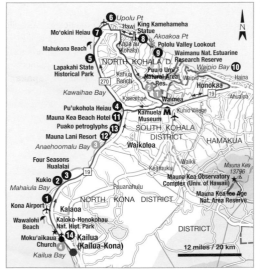

run by a young Waimea couple that knows food. After you've refueled, stop at the eclectic **Kamuela Museum** (www.kamuela museum.com), on the west side of town for a little bit of, well, everything. It's a bit like you're in someone's attic.

Should beach-time summon, it's but a short drive back to South Kohala and Kona. Otherwise, continue east on Route 19 to Hono-kaa and the **Waipi'o Valley Lookout at Waipio Bay ❿**, 1,000ft (305 meters) above the transcendent valley, at one time inhabited by thousands.

Puako petroglyphs

Art stops

Turn back towards Waimea and through to the Queen K. Heading south again, visit the **Mauna Kea Beach Hotel** ⑪, whose Asian and Pacific art collection is as magnificent as its crescent beach. Turn in at **Mauna Lani Resort** ⑫ (see page 92) and follow the signs to the **Puako petroglyphs** ⑬, where you'll find fascinating ancient rock drawings representing scenes of life in pre-contact Hawai'i.

Refuel

Ready for an Oceanside snack, drink, or simply a place to sit in the shade? Skip the big resorts at Waikoloa and head to **Lava Lava Beach Club**, see ③, for a taste of old Hawai'i – charming cottages, a restaurant and seats in the sand. Continue back to Kona, the leeward side's largest town is the island's social hotspot. On Ali'i Drive, you'll find **Moku'aikaua Church** ⑭, built in 1837. Sunset is free along the harbor seawall. Add dinner to the view at **Huggo's**, see ④, if you're back in time.

Food and Drink

① MERRIMAN'S

65-1227 Opelo Road; tel: 808-885 6822; www.merrimanshawaii.com; Mon–Fri 11.30am–1.30pm, 5.30–9pm, Sat–Sun 10am–1pm, 5.30–9pm; $$$–$$$$

People have been known to travel from neighbor islands just to dine at Merriman's. Known for its regional cuisine, chef-owner Peter Merriman is a product of the resorts who, thankfully, stepped out on his own. Expect fresh locally grown food with a Hawaiian twist.

② PAU RESTAURANT

65-1227 Opelo Road; tel: 808-885 6325; www.paupizza.com; daily 11am–8pm; $$

Pau's signature lunch dish is a fresh fish sandwich cooked to perfection on a soft ciabatta bun with lettuce, tomato and tartar sauce – the salad it comes with was grown right in Waimea.

③ LAVA LAVA BEACH CLUB

69-1091 Ku'uali'i Place; tel: 808-769 5282; www.lavalavabeachclub.com; daily 11am–9pm; $$–$$$

Both a small cottage resort and restaurant, Lava Lava offers a fun, toes in the sand, laid-back luxury experience. While inside seating is an option, where else can you sit at a table in the sand and shade while enjoying shrimp and fried rice in a carved out pineapple? It doesn't get any more Hawai'i than this.

④ HUGGO'S

75-5828 Kahakai Road; tel: 808-329 1493; www.huggos.com; dining Sun–Thu 5.30pm–9pm, Fri–Sat 5.30–10pm, cocktail lounge Mon–Thu 4–10pm, Fri–Sun 5pm–midnight; $$

Huggo's is literally perched on the rocks just off Kona's Ali'i Drive. Come for the views of sunset, but know that the food will be just as good. Fresh seafood here truly is fresh.

Garden of the Gods trail on Lanai

MOLOKAI AND LANAI

Island-hopping is part of the full Hawai'i experience. If you like resort life and are content to spend your time lounging by the pool or snorkeling with dolphins, then Lanai is the best option. On the other hand, if you can live without the creature comforts and want to explore Hawai'i's 'wild west', then Molokai is the one to go for.

DISTANCE: N/A – air or boat travel required
TIME: A day trip, or 1–2 days
START: Kahalui Airport (Molokai or Lanai), Lahaina's Pioneer Inn (Lanai only)
END: Lanai City, Lanai; Kaunakakai, Molokai
POINTS TO NOTE: Lanai is best for a single day trip via ferry from Lahaina or flight from any of the island's airports, and Molokai is best seen over two or three days. On both, expect quiet roads, empty beaches and small towns.

LANAI

Thought by ancient Polynesians to be ghost stomping grounds and thus best avoided, Lanai's red volcanic earth later proved fertile for pineapples, the economic backbone of this island, now mostly owned by Oracle-founder Larry Ellison. Two luxury hotels dominate the tourist market on Lanai: **Manele Bay Resort ❶** with a Mediterranean-Hawaiian ambiance, and **The Lodge at Koele ❷**, with fireplaces and an Old World character.

Travel

Accessible by plane and boats from Maui, including one-day snorkeling trips, Lanai is the perfect place if you truly wish to do nothing but lie on the beach or by the pool, or play golf. The spinner dolphins come into Manele Bay and delight in playing with the snorkelers almost every morning, and dining at the resort of your choice is best. In addition to short but pricey flights, the ferry leaves Lahaina for Lanai at 6.45am, 9.15am, 12.45pm, 3.15pm and 5.45pm, and comes back to Maui at 8am, 10.30am, 2pm, 4.30pm and 6.45pm. Tickets can be purchased in advance (www.go-lanai.com).

If you're considering sightseeing beyond the hotels on Lanai, you'll need to rent an off-road vehicle. From centrally located Lanai City, **Kaiolohia Beach ❸**, home to an offshore shipwreck eerily sitting on the reef, is a

Shipwreck off Kaiolohia Beach

30-minute drive. Take Highway 44 to the very end, then turn left and follow the dirt/sand road to the parking area, then hike along the beach towards the shipwreck. Once there, look for the old lighthouse foundation on the beach (a patch of concrete), then follow a trail south from there. White paint marks the trail. Just a few hundred feet into the trail, **petroglyphs** will be visible on the right – look, but please don't touch the ancient art.

MOLOKAI

Larger and geographically more diverse, Molokai is a good island for exploration. It has wide open grasslands, moody rain forests, wild deer, and on the north shore, the world's tallest ocean cliffs.

Accomodations and restaurants

The best accommodations are at Paniolo Hale in **Kaluakoi** ❹, on the gorgeous and empty long white beaches of west Molokai. Look for rentals from private owners online. **Papohaku Beach** ❺, just south of the west Molokai condos, is more than 2 miles (3km) long and nearly always empty. This is beachcombing at its best – shells are untouched and waiting to be plucked from the sand. The once-bustling Molokai Ranch has shut down, and the Kaluakoi Hotel & Golf Club has gone fallow, providing only a shell of a resort and a ghost town feel.

There are very few restaurants on Molokai, but head into **Kaunakakai** ❻, the island's largest town (about four blocks long), for the Li Hing Mui

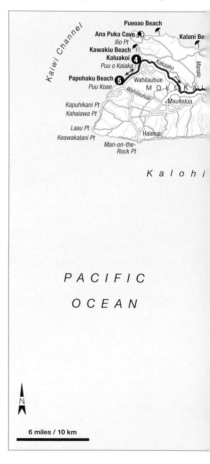

Plumeria trees on Molokai

Storefronts in Kaunakakai

Margarita and Saimin (Japanese-style noodle soup) at **Paddler's Inn**, see ❶, or pizza at the **Molokai Pizza Café**, see ❷.

East Molokai and Halawa Valley

From Kaunakakai, travel along the coast dotted with ancient Hawaiian Fishponds all the way to the east-

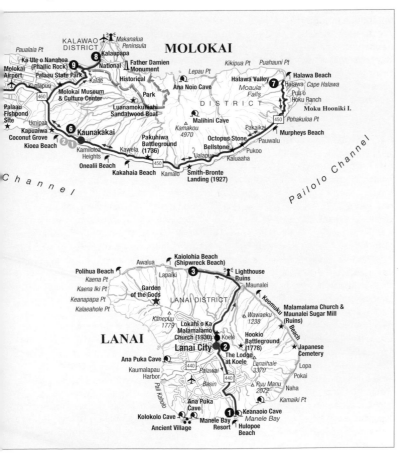

Kaluapapa mule trek

ern tip at **Halawa Valley** ❼. Visit the beach, but skip the waterfall trail – the family at the far end of the beach runs a years-long scam, hostily demanding money for your presence on 'their' land.

Kalaupapa

Tour operators infest Hawai'i, but there is a tour worth visiting Molokai alone for, as it humbles you with modern Hawai'i's saddest but most grace-ful episode: **Kalaupapa** ❽, the former leprosy colony on Makanalua Peninsula, isolated from the rest of Molokai by 2,000ft (610-meter) -high cliffs and dangerous ocean waters. Starting in the early 1800s, Oahu health authorities shipped over 10,000 people – anybody with leprosy, now called Hansen's disease, and often those with nothing more than a bad skin rash, to Kalaupapa for a life sentence of exile. The 1873 arrival of Joseph De Veuster from Belgium, better known as Father Damien, brought civility and dignity to Kalaupapa. He later contracted and died of Hansen's disease. Protected by the National Park Service, the community has fewer than 10 remaining patients, all of whom could leave, but choose to stay.

You can either be invited to visit Kalaupapa, or you can join the Molokai Mule Ride (www.muleride.com). If you fly in or hike in, you'll still need an escort once you reach Kalaupapa. Permission can be obtained through the state department of health in Honolulu or Molokai. Children under 16 are not allowed on the peninsula. To simply see the site from above, follow the road back through Kaunakakai, taking Route 470 north to the end of the road. The overlook provides a stunning view to the peninsula below. Before leaving, follow the signs from the parking lot to **Phallic Rock** ❾. As you might guess, it makes for an unforgettable photo opportunity.

Food and Drink

❶ PADDLER'S INN

10 Mohala Street; tel: 808-553 3300; www.molokaipaddlersinn.com; 11am–late; $–$$

Paddler's Inn isn't exactly the only restaurant in town, but it's the best – not only for the food and drink, but for truly reflecting the small town feel and *aloha* of Molokai. Images of paddling teams and fish caught line the bamboo-veneered walls, and live music plays in the evenings.

❷ MOLOKAI PIZZA CAFÉ

15 Kaunakakai Place, Kaunakakai; tel: 808-553 3288; L, D daily; $–$$

In addition to serving pizza (as the name suggests), this restaurant offers a mean prime rib and surprisingly good Mexican food. The atmosphere is casual and fun; at times, even on sparsely populated Molokai, it can actually feel lively.

Salt spray crashes upon Ali'i Drive in Kailua Bay

SOUTH KONA AND SOUTH POINT

Journey to the southernmost point of the US, a desolate rocky point that feels like another planet, but first, snorkel in some of the clearest water in Hawai'i, tasting your way down the coffee-growing coast through South Kona's sleepy, artsy towns.

DISTANCE: 149 miles (240km) roundtrip
TIME: A full day
START: Ali'i Drive, Kona
END: Holualoa Town
POINTS TO NOTE: Pack the sunscreen, as you'll spend as much time exposed to the sun as you do in the car on this tour. You'll need at least $50 cash per person to ensure you can rent a kayak in the very casual commerce at Kealakekua Bay. Tandem kayaks are a good option for families with kids who can swim.

SOUTH KONA

Leaving Kona from **Ali'i Drive ❶**, head up Palani Road to the Queen Kaahumanu Highway (see page 50) and follow it south until the highway merges with Mamalahoa Highway at Honalo. Do like the *kama'aina* and stop for breakfast at family-run **Teshima's** on the left, see ❶. Down the road in the town of Captain Cook proper is the **Manago Hotel**, see ❷, where the menu is simple and cheap, and known for its lip-smacking pork chops.

Kealakekua Bay

Makai of town (towards the ocean) is **Kealakekua Bay ❷**, a state marine conservation district and the site of Captain Cook's 1779 dismemberment by insulted Hawaiians. At the bayfront, haggle for a rental kayak with local vendors ($30–60) and paddle to the 27ft (8-meter) -high monument on British territory solemnizing Cook. Have your snorkeling gear handy to hop in with the spinner dolphins that are always curious and friendly. Jump in at the monument to experience coral colors and fish like nowhere else in Hawai'i.

Coffee country

All along the highway south of Kona, fresh Kona coffee is sold. Head into any store for a taste, but forget the blends as they're only 10 percent pure Kona. Head back up to Mamalahoa after your swim, then take the turnoff to **Pu'uhonua 'O Honaunau National Historical Park ❸**. Meticulously and accurately restored, it was an ancient refuge where transgressors and *kapu violaters* were pardoned by priests – but only after out-swimming sharks or scaling stone walls, and vowing to do

Grounds of Pu'uhonua 'O Honaunau National Historic Park

penance. The grounds are wonderful for idle walking and inspecting the full-sized primitive idols and the Great Wall. On the way back to the main road, stop at the 20th-century St Benedict's Church. The inside of the church is painted with biblical scenes and motifs.

Coffee plants and macadamia nut trees give way further south to barren black nothingness – lava flows from 1907, 1919, 1926 and 1950. Take the turn off for **South Point ❹**. The road is paved, although it is narrow, winding and steep. South Point is compelling and powerful. Enjoy the view from the cliff edge near the Kalalea Heiau, where clear blue waters crash against the basalt cliffs.

Sleepy, artsy Holualoa

Backtrack along Mamalahoa Highway towards Kona, and exploring the fishing village of **Miloli'i ❺** and the hillside artist's town of **Holualoa ❻**, above Kailua-Kona. Look out for the Kimura Lauhala Shop, Kona Art Center and the unique and beautiful art of M. Field, which decorates walls, surfboards, paddles and clothing. The charming town has an art walk with food and drinks the first Friday evening of every month.

Food and Drink

❶ TESHIMA'S

79-7251 Mamalahoa Highway; tel: 808-322 9140; www.teshimarestaurant.com; daily 6.30am–1.45pm and 5–9pm; $
Grandma Teshima's mission was excellent food and service in a comfortable atmosphere and that's exactly what this place offers. Try the tempura and sashimi.

❷ MANAGO HOTEL

82-6151 Mamalahoa Highway; tel: 808-323 2642; www.managohotel.com/rest.html; Tue–Sun 7–9am, 11am–2pm, 5–7.30pm; $
They're as proud of their pork chop as they are of the fact that everything on the menu costs less than $15. Food is simple, hearty and a welcome break from the land of $10-plus cocktails further north.

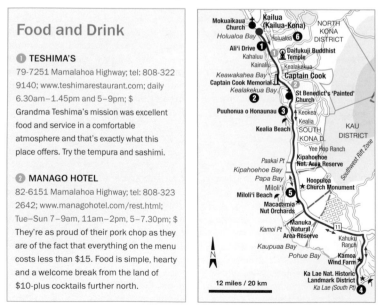

Anthuriums at Hilo Farmer's Market

HILO

Hilo is among Hawai'i's biggest secrets. It gets more than 120ins (305cm) of rain annually, making it green, lush and full of waterfalls – even in downtown. You'll meet residents along this tour who have never even bothered to leave the island, and who are admirably committed to supporting local agriculture and the economy.

DISTANCE: 9 miles (14km) driving, 2 miles (3km) walking
TIME: 2–3 hours
START: Hilo Airport
END: Hilo Bay Café
POINTS TO NOTE: Fly in to the Hilo Airport directly from a neighbor island, or drive from Kona over the improved Saddle Road, which takes you through the heart of the Big Island. If coming from Waimea, you'll see the beautiful, rugged Hamakua Coast – allow an extra hour for the drive along the coast. Pack a poncho, because it rains nearly every day in Hilo. There's enough to do to spend a day or three, and the drive from the more touristy Kona side is long – sometimes more than two hours.

First impressions of Hilo, the government seat of Hawai'i County, often underwhelm. Hawai'i's second-largest city outside Oahu, Hilo feels more like a big town, which it really is. It certainly harbors no pretenses in humoring the tourist, and thus its charm. Hilo's focus is the harbor. Tsunamis – or tidal waves – in 1946 and 1960 destroyed part of the downtown business district and claimed many lives, but many of the old buildings remain.

From the **airport ❶**, which is close, but not right in it, drive into Hilo via Route 19, Kamehameha Avenue, to Mamo Street. Left onto Mamo Street puts you right in the heart of **Hilo's Farmer's Market ❷** (www.hilofarmers market.com; Sun–Tue and Thu–Fri 7am–4pm, Wed and Sat 6am–4pm), one of the best in the state, especially on Wednesdays and Saturdays when more than 200 vendors are present. You'll find avocados and papayas bigger than your head, local homemade products and gifts, all for great prices. Take your time wandering the stalls, where samples abound – you'll likely leave feeling like you had lunch.

From the farmer's market, leave the car behind and walk along Kamehameha Avenue's charming storefronts. The **Pacific Tsunami Museum ❸** (www.tsunami.org; Tue–Sat 10am–

Vegetation near Rainbow Falls

4pm) captures the devastation caused by the two tsunamis that are integral to this town's history. While heartbreaking, it's also very well done and informative. Local designer **Sig Zane's shop ❹** is among the most popular – local men wear these *aloha* shirts across the state for business attire. Even the Governor and Mayor are often seen sporting Sig Zane's shirts.

For another taste of locally created food and wares, continue north on Kamehameha Avenue to **Locavore**, see ❶, an eclectic mix of gifts and treats all made in the Hilo-Hamakua area. Just up the street, the **Hilo Town Tavern**, see ❷, which features live music in the evenings and draws in the locals, is the real deal – this is where Hilo folks come to unwind. Pop in for a beer and to make new friends.

Travel south on Keawe Street until you reach Haili Street, then turn right and walk to the **Lyman House Memo-**

rial Museum and Mission House ❺ (www.lymanmuseum.org; Mon–Sat 10am–4.30pm; Mission House tours at 11am and 2pm). The museum's first floor is dedicated to Hawaiiana. Upstairs is the secret treasure: world-class rock and mineral, and shell collections. In the museum's gift shop, pick up an inexpensive walking tour map of old Hilo.

Take the short walk back to your car, and pop over to **Rainbow Falls ❻** – Hilo really does have a waterfall right in town! Follow Kamehameha Road north to Waianuenue Road (Route 200), go left and follow it to Rainbow Drive. The waterfall will be on your right. The waterfall ranges from a trickle on dry days, to a raging river when it's raining in the mountains above.

After visiting the falls, travel back to Kamehameha Avenue and follow it south along the bay, making a left onto Banyon Drive. This is **Hilo's hotel**

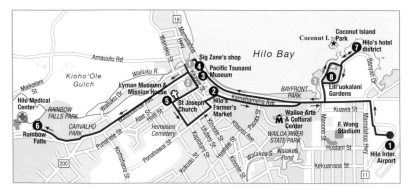

View of the Pacific from Route 11

district ❼, with the very modestly priced Hawai'i Naniloa and the Hilo Hawaiian both offering comfortable, if slightly shabby, accommodations along with excellent coastal views. Opposite is **Lili'uokalani Gardens** ❽, an uncrowded, serene Japanese garden of stone bridges and lions, lanterns and a tea ceremony pavilion. Park the car and walk the gardens out to the point, finishing up at **Hilo Bay Café**, see ❸, for a meal with a view so stunning you may forget to eat. Ask for an outside table in the shade, and whatever the fish special is, order it.

South of Hilo is a splendid scenic drive down Highway 130 towards the coast and recent lava flows, and Route 11 connects to Route 10, through Volcanoes National Park (see page 62). Hilo is the closest town with accommodations outside the park.

Rainbow Falls

Food and Drink

❶ LOCAVORE

60 Kamehameha Avenue; tel: 808-965 2372; www.bigislandlocavorestore.com; Mon–Fri 9am–6pm, Sat 9am–3pm; $$
Locavore is not a restaurant per se, but there's plenty to eat in this grocery/deli/shop. Absolutely everything here is fresh and local, so you can't go wrong for a midday snack or lunch overlooking the bay.

❷ HILO TOWN TAVERN

168 Keawe Street; tel: 808-935 2171; www.hilotowntavern.com; pupus and drinks $–$$
The Hilo Town Tavern is the only place in town when it comes to nightlife. Check out open mic night (Monday) and various DJs and local live music while enjoying libations with the locals.

❸ HILO BAY CAFÉ

123 Lihiwai Street; tel: 808-935 4939; www.hilobaycafe.com; Mon–Thu 11am–9pm, Fri–Sat 11am–9.30pm; $$–$$$
Here you'll find Hilo's fanciest fare, with fresh caught ocean fish, hand-rolled sushi and artisan cocktails. Reservations are recommended.

Gas and smoke rise from Halema'uma'u Crater

HAWAI'I VOLCANOES NATIONAL PARK

Tour an active volcano, complete with flowing lava, smelly vapors and cool misty forests of trees unlike any others in the world. If you're truly lucky, you'll get such a good view that you just might find your rubber-soled shoes begin to melt.

DISTANCE: 40 miles (64km)
TIME: A full day or more
START: Hawai'i Volcanoes National Park Visitor Center
END: Volcano Village
POINTS TO NOTE: The weather can be a bit cool at the top of the park, but layers of clothing are the best solution – the coastline, which can bring you much nearer to flowing lava, is as hot as you'd expect it to be. Covered shoes are a must. Although you can push for half a day, this option really deserves a full day, or better yet, two. This tour is suitable for children – it's a wonderful park for all ages. If you wish to take your time exploring, a stay in Hilo or Volcano Village is a good option.

First things first – to truly understand the geological force you're standing upon, start at the **Hawai'i Volcanoes National Park Visitor Center ❶**. Not only will you learn about the volcano, you'll also get information you need on road closures and volcanic activity information. Ask the staff if you can view the flowing lava along the coast today – and heed their advice.

Kilauea

The park celebrated its 100th birthday in 2016. Across the road from the visitor center is **Volcano House ❷**, a hotel and restaurant perched on the very rim of **Kilauea Caldera ❸**. All of the current volcanic activity is from Kilauea, which is the longest continuously erupting volcano in the world. Volcano House's location is superb, and its caldera lookout is a must; varying hues of lava on the caldera bottom betray multiple lava flows between 1885 and 1982. The rooms are comfortable, though basic, and the hotel dining room offers decent fare for dinner. Cross the road to the **Volcano Art Center ❹**, next to the visitor center is rich in creative talent, and the center's offerings are perhaps some of the best in the islands.

This is the realm of Pele, the volcano goddess. From the visitor center, follow Crater Rim Drive. A few min-

Chain of Craters Road   *Lava field*

utes past Steaming Bluff, where seeping groundwater hits hot rock. Drive across a 1974 lava flow to the **Halema'uma'u Lookout ⑤**. The short path is sometimes veiled in smelly vapors; note the signs and health warnings. Halema'uma'u, a collapsed crater within Kilauea Caldera, is said to be the current abode of Pele. Believers leave gifts of *ti* leaves, coins and flower *leis* on the rim. It's considered very bad luck to take lava rock from the island – the visitor's center features letters of those that have sent it back.

Loihi

Turn off on to the Chain of Craters Road, which descends down Kilauea's East Rift (which itself descends into the ocean). A new island-to-be, Loihi, gestates 3,000ft (915 meters) below the surface on the east rift and is probably 100,000 years from reaching the surface. Once it was possible to loop around to Hilo this back way through

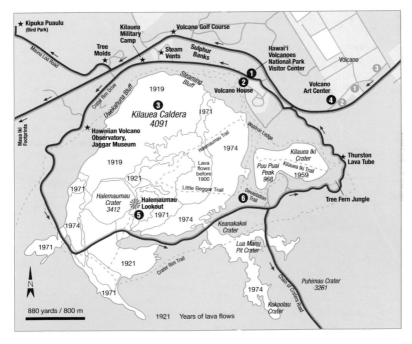

the village of Kalapana, but Pele, ever a force to be reckoned with, changed all that when flowing lava destroyed the town and road.

Viewing lava

When lava flows hit the ocean, spiraling clouds of steam rise furiously hundreds of feet into the air. Twilight turns the coast into a strangely beautiful and surreal red perdition. Check with the visitor center about hiking out – if they say it's a go, do so in the evening for the best views. Returning to the rim road, drive past the Kilauea Iki Crater. In 1959, a 2,000ft (610-meter) -high fountain issued skyward from here. The **Devastation Trail** ⑥ is a somber meditation, countered by a rainforest walk to, and through, the Thurston Lava Tube. Other surprises demand your time: Kipuka Pua'ulu (Bird Park), the Tree Molds and the Mauna Iki Footprints. As Kamehameha I was consolidating his rule over the Big Island, some fleeing warriors died on the Ka'u Desert from Kilauea's toxic gases and their footprints solidified in the ash. It's an easy trail, one of many that slice through the park.

Food and drink

Volcano Village is just minutes from the park entrance. A lot of artists have gravitated to this 3,700ft elevation (1,128-meter) community, which is a quiet, reflective place. The best food can be found at **Café Ohia**, see ①, **Volcano House**, see ② or the **Kilauea Lodge**, see ③. Several excellent bed-and-breakfast options are also in the area.

Food and Drink

① CAFÉ OHIA

19-4005 Haunani Road, Volcano; tel: 808-985 8587; www.cafeohia.blogspot.com; daily 6am–7pm; $

This is a cute little shop with outdoor picnic table seating only. Maybe not for the committed carnivore, but not vegetarian either. Try the daily special – they know what they're doing!

② VOLCANO HOUSE

Crater Rim Drive; tel: 808-756 9625; www.hawaiivolcanohouse.com/dining; 7am–10am, 11am–2pm and 5.30–9pm; $$

This place overlooks Kilauea Crater and serves dishes made from locally sourced meats, fruit and veggies, making for wonderful, hearty meals.

③ KILAUEA LODGE

19-3948 Old Volcano Road, Volcano; tel: 808-967 7366; www.kilauealodge.com; 7.30am–2pm, dinner from 5pm, Sunday Brunch 10am–2pm; $$$–$$$$

This place has a cozy, mountain-cabin feel and a full range of dishes – from comfort food to fine dining – to delight every guest.

Artists' studio in Hanapepe

WAIMEA CANYON AND WEST KAUAI

The further west you go, the redder the earth and the bigger the cliffs and beaches get. At the top of Waimea Canyon you'll get to view Kalalau Valley the easy way. As this itinerary reaches high altitudes, take a warm jacket or sweater.

DISTANCE: 60 miles (100km)
TIME: A full day
START: Koloa Town
END: Polihale Beach
POINTS TO NOTE: Waimea Canyon is a hiker's dream – if you're ambitious, fit and truly want the best view of Na Pali Coast available, wear your hiking shoes and bring a day pack with snacks and water. The road up the canyon twists and turns, best to sit in front or drive if prone to carsickness. Children will love Koke'e Lodge's chickens and looking for goats on the canyon walls.

WEST KAUAI

Koloa

Hit the road early for this route, and skip the hotel buffet. A number of places en route encourage exploratory nibbling. **Old Koloa Town ❶**, a few minutes up the road from Poipu, was once a sugar town but is now home to an enjoyable mix of shops and restaurants. Stop in for your coffee at **Lap-**pert's Ice Cream, see ❶, then hit **Sueoka's**, see ❷, a family-run store since 1933, to stock up on snacks for the long trip. The chimney across the street is the only remnant of Hawai'i's first sugar mill. From Koloa, Route 520 leads you through the tree tunnel and to the main island highway, Route 50, where sugar cane fields climb right up to the foothills on your right as you head west.

West Kauai Towns

A veil of clouds up at 5,147ft (1,600 meters), is **Mount Wai'ale'ale ❷**. It gets a *minimum* of 450ins (1,143cm) of rain annually and is rarely visible. Drive past residential Ele'ele to Port Allen and pull in at **Grinds Café**, see ❸, for Kauai coffee and sweet breakfast treats, served all day long. A couple of blinks beyond, watch for **Hanapepe ❸** and turn into town. Hanapepe shows its age but art is alive in this town. Art lovers should pop in to the several galleries in old storefronts.

Further west, the ruins of **Fort Elizabeth ❹** recall a fascinating episode in

Hawai'i's history. In 1815, a Russian ship wrecked near Waimea, and Kaua'i's king claimed its cargo. An agent of the czar was sent to negotiate return

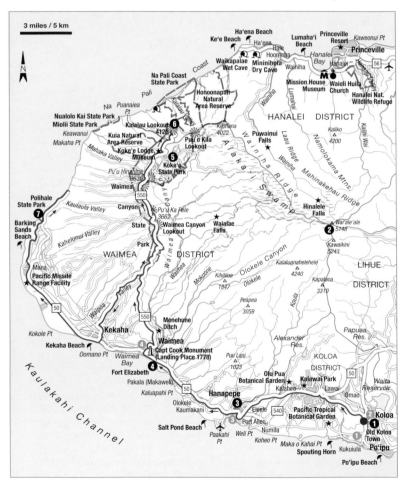

3 miles / 5 km

N

Ha'ena Beach
Ke'e Beach
Ha'ena
Hale
Hoomaha
Lumaha'i Beach
Princeville Resort
Kaweonui Pt
Princeville
56

Na Pali Coast State Park
Coast
Waikapalae Wet Cave
Mininihofa Dry Cave
Wainiha
Hanalei Bay
Hanalei

Mission House Museum
Waioli Huiia Church
Hanalei Nat. Wildlife Refuge

Honoonapali Natural Area Reserve

Na
Puanaiea Pt
Pali
Kalalau Pdwy

HANALEI DISTRICT

Kaliko
4200

Nualolo Kai State Park
Miolii State Park
Keawanui
Makaha Pt
Kalalau Lookout 4120
Kuia Natural Area Reserve
Koke'e Lodge, Museum
Pu'u o Kila Lookout
6
5
Koke'e State Park
Kilohana 4022
Puwainui Falls
Alakai Swamp
Wainiha Ridge
Laau Ridge
Namolokama Mtns
Mahinakehau Ridge

Mahaka Valley
Pu'u Hinahina 3636
Waimea
550
Canyon
State

Polihale State Park
7
Barking Sands Beach
Kaulaula Valley
Kahelunui Valley
Pu'u Ka Pele 3662
Waimea Canyon Lookout
Waialae Falls
Hinalele Falls
Wai'ale'ale 5148
2

WAIMEA
Park
DISTRICT
Waimea
Mokuone
Kawaikini 5243

Mana
Pacific Missile Range Facility
Waipoa
550
Olokele Canyon
Kihilioa 1847
Olokele
Kalaluanahelehele 4240
LIHUE DISTRICT

50
Kokole Pt
Kekaha
Menehune Ditch
Waimea
Peapea 3059
Kolula
Kapaloa 3310
Papuaa Res.

Kekaha Beach
Oomano Pt
4
Capt Cook Monument (Landing Place 1778)
4
Waimea Bay
Fort Elizabeth
Alexander Res.
Pu'u Lani 1023
Olu Pua Botanical Garden
Kalawai Park
KOLOA DISTRICT
50
Waita Reservoir

Kaulakahi Channel
Pakala (Makaweli)
Kaluapahi Pt
Olokele
Kaumakani
50
Hanapepe
3
Eleele
540
Kalahea
Lawai
Omao
Koloa
2
1

Salt Pond Beach
Paakahi Pt
Weli Pt
Port Allen
3
Numila
Koheo Pt
Pacific Tropical Botanical Garden
Maka o Kahai Pt
Spouting Horn
Kukuiula
1
Old Koloa Town
Po'ipu
Po'ipu Beach

Waimea Canyon

of the valuable cargo. He got carried away and tried to negotiate for a slice of Hawai'i as well. Construction began in 1816 but never finished. Continue to Waimea Bay, where Captain Cook made his first Hawaiian landfall in 1778; an unassuming statue of Cook acknowledges the event.

WAIMEA CANYON

In Waimea, turn inland onto Waimea Canyon Road, but before you get too far, stop at **Yumi's**, see ④. The window says 'sushi and pies', but inside heavenly cinnamon rolls await. Waimea Canyon Road lumbers upward, eventually yielding to stunning views of the canyon. There are several lookouts where you can watch mists, rainbows, shadows and colors shift in this 3,500ft (1,060-meter) deep, 10-mile (16km) -long chasm. Pass **Koke'e State Park** ⑤ (don't worry – you'll come back!) and head to spectacular views from **Kalalau Lookout** ⑥ along the 4,000ft (1,200-meter) rim of Kalalau Valley. If the view is hidden by clouds, wait a few minutes. It's best in the morning. The swooping valley drops down to a beautiful beach, the terminus of an 11-mile (17km) trail originating at the other end of the Na Pali Coast, near Hanalei (see page 71).

Koke'e Lodge
Swing back to Koke'e State Park, a refuge for many of Hawai'i's indigenous and endangered birds, and haven to hundreds of wild chickens. Koke'e Lodge has a dozen rustic cabins.

Ni'ihau

The flat-topped island visible off the west coast of Kauai is Ni'ihau, the westernmost of the seven inhabited Hawaiian Islands, and home to 130 native Hawaiians. The island is privately-owned by the Robinson Family and access has been limited since 1915. Living largely by traditional means, residents of Ni'ihau speak Hawaiian primarily, and rarely leave the island. When they do so, it's usually to visit relatives on Kauai. Relatively few people are allowed to visit, and most are related to the Robinsons, although hunting excursions are sometimes allowed to help control eland, aoudad and oryx, and wild sheep and boars.

For reasons that are clear, the island is sometimes called 'The Forbidden Isle'. Some residents do own televisions, but service is limited. There is one school on the island, Ni'ihau School. While traveling, you'll often see Ni'ihau shell *lei*, more like necklaces than actual *lei*, sold for top dollar in hotel and museum gift shops. These are made up of tiny shells that wash up on shores of the island in the winter, and are an important source of revenue for island residents.

Polihale State Park

Stop at the museum for a brief on the area's natural history, and for walking and hiking information. For the avid hiker, the strenuous Awa'awapuhi trail offers stunning views of Na Pali Coast. Hike in and out, or loop back on Nulolo Trail.

POLIHALE

Follow the road back down to the coast, keeping right at the fork. At the bottom, drive through Kekaha, past the rundown sugar mill and onto Route 50. At the road's end, **Polihale State Park ❼** will surprise you with a sprawling sandy beach and a new view of Na Pali cliffs. Follow the signs – it's unpaved, but 4WD isn't necessary. Forget about swimming at Polihale, with its unpredictable currents, and enjoy beachcombing instead. Polihale and neighboring beach Barking Sands make up the longest continuous beach in all of Hawai'i. Polihale is a favorite camping site for local families; don't be surprised to see them driving their 4x4s onto the sand here. Don't try it, as you need to adjust tire pressure and you'll likely get stuck. Curious about that flat-top island across the way? It's **Ni'ihau**, inhabited, Hawaiian-speaking and no tourists allowed (see box).

Food and Drink

❶ LAPPERT'S HAWAI'I

2829 Ala Kalanikaumaka Street; tel: 808-742 1272; www.lappertshawaii.com; daily 6am–10pm; $
Locally created Lappert's Ice Cream has unique flavors of ice cream that capture Kauai in a cone. Coffee is fresh roasted and the perfect pairing.

❷ SEUOKA'S

5392 Koloa Road, Koloa; tel: 808-742 1611; www.sueokastore.com; daily B, L, D; $
Seuoka's is a local grocer with a snack shop/food counter on the side that locals line up for. Try the plate lunch – choose your favorite meat, and dive in.

❸ GRINDS CAFÉ

4469 Waialo Road in the shopping center; tel: 808-335 6027; www.grindscafe.net; B, L Mon 5.30–9pm, Tue–Thu 6am–3pm, Fri–Sun 5.30am–9pm; $
Serves breakfast all day. Try the walnut cinnamon roll, even if you're just driving by. Hearty portions at this down-home diner.

❹ YUMI'S

9691 Kaumualii Highway; tel: 808-338 1731; Tue–Thu 7am–2.30pm, Fri 7am–1pm and 6–8pm, Sat 8am–1pm; $
Yumi's in Waimea serves breakfast all day, but is known for the burger and *loco moco* – a local delight that includes a burger patty, fried egg, rice and gravy.

Kilauea Point Lighthouse

HANALEI AND KAUAI'S NORTH SHORE

A day-trip to the majestic north shore of Kauai, over one-lane bridges to cliffs, waterfalls, quaint little towns and lighthouses. Consider spending a night – or several – movie stars and CEOs have been known to come here and never leave again.

DISTANCE: 77 miles (124km)
TIME: A full day
START: Lihue
END: Hanalei
POINTS TO NOTE: Heed all signs – the beaches are stunning and tempting, but signs are there for good reason. Shorebreak can be rough during the winter months. Pack your swimsuit, hiking shoes and snorkeling gear – even in the winter there are calm days.

NORTH SHORE BOUND

Start north on Highway 56 (Kuhio Highway) from Lihue as early as you can for this big day out. Continue through Wailua (see page 78). **Poli'ahu Heiau** and **Opaeka'a Falls ❶** are quick visits en route, which are worth the jaunt up the hill. Beyond Wailua is Kapa'a, a humming local town – avoid trying to drive back through between 3pm and 6pm, as traffic on the narrow highway road comes to a standstill. **Java Kai**, see ❶, on the ocean side, is a nice stop for coffee and breakfast.

KILAUEA AND THE LIGHTHOUSE

Leaving Kapa'a, you'll find the beautiful but dangerous **Kealia Beach ❷** (otherwise known as Donkey Beach), great for a walk and for watching the surfers. Push on, there's much ahead. Pass through the small town of Anahola (blink and you'll miss it – that post office, general store and burger joint *are* the town), and follow the coast up to **Kilauea ❸**, a quaint village known for its lighthouse and wildlife refuge. Turn right into Kilauea Road and follow signs toward the lighthouse. Turn right on Keneke Street to find **Kilauea Bakery and Pau Hana Pizza**, see ❷, and pick up some baked goods for the road. The best eclectic mix of art and shopping in the state is in the beautiful lava rock building built in 1881 on the corner of Kilauea and Keneke roads at Kong Lum. You'll find treasures for everyone on your list – including yourself.

The lighthouse at **Kilauea Point National Wildlife Refuge ❹** (www.fws. gov/refuge/Kilauea_Point; Tue–Sat 10am–4pm; children free) is known for the world's largest clamshell lens and gor-

Hanalei Valley Lookout

geous views of the coast and seabirds riding the wind. Look out for the frigate bird, with its 8ft (2-meter) wingspan; the Nene (Hawai'i's State Bird) and the laysan albatross that nests here, having instinctually returned to its birthplace to lay its egg. Scan the ocean 700ft (210 meters) below for turtles, whales, rays and dolphins.

PRINCEVILLE

Past Kilauea, the highway roles through gentle countryside with views of the island's mountainous interior. Princeville, named after Kamehameha IV's son, Prince Albert, is home to mainland transplants and retirees, as well as the Princeville St. Regis. Take note and pop in later for a ginger margarita and a final glimpse of waterfall-surrounded Hanalei Bay on your way back to town. Princeville is the last gas station you'll pass, so take this opportunity to fill up. They're the only one on the north shore, so you'll pay a premium.

HANALEI

On the main highway beyond the Princeville entrance is the **Hanalei Valley Lookout ❺**. Hanalei provides half of Hawai'i's poi supply from the traditionally cultivated taro fields below. The lower extent of Hanalei Valley also serves as a national wildlife refuge. Below, the 1913 vintage one-lane bridge, cherished by local residents in spite of the wait, carries you across to Hanalei.

Hanalei is home to a mix of *kama 'aina*, surfers, new age types and celebrities in hiding, and more than its fair share of beach bums. Don't be fooled – the 'simple-living' folks here are living in homes that start at a million dollars. The **Hanalei Dolphin**, see ❸, takes advantage of its riverside setting that makes alfresco dining an option and the fish tastes like it may have been swimming this morning.

The main commercial center is **Ching Young Village ❻**, good for bee pollen, *The New York Times*, surf style clothes or camping gear. Across the street find more shops, including the beach-house decor staple Sand People, as well as **Hanalei Gourmet**, see ❹, a deli that offers eclectic fare with a Hawaiian regional twist, a casual atmosphere and live music on select nights. Down the road on the left is a New England-looking green church. This is the **Wai'oli Hui'ia Church ❼**, more easily pronounced 'the green church'. Stop in and take a peak – paired with the view of the valley behind it, with the always-running Namolokama Falls at the center, it's a picturesque rest stop.

BEYOND HANALEI

The road from Hanalei to the end of civilization winds through mountain streams and one-lane bridges, passing beautiful empty beaches and simple stilt houses on multi-million-dollar plots of land. The road begins to twist and shoot past **Lumaha'i Beach ❽**, made famous in the musical *South Pacific*. A truly beauti-

Hanalei   *Bridge over the Wailua River near Hanalei*

ful beach, it is flanked by black lava rock. Despite its daytime popularity, it's often empty at sunset. Park at the trailhead at the north/west end of Hanalei Bay and take the short, five-minute hike down for a look.

Around Ha'ena Beach are several wet and dry caves that are actually ancient lava tubes, some extending a mile back – it's worth pulling off the road to have a look. Another couple of miles further, as the road gets narrower, is the end of the road and **Ke'e Beach** ❾. Midday

is crowded here, but the snorkeling is unbeatable in summer. Join the crowds and snorkel along the mountains edge and out for a glimpse of Na Pali Coast from the water. Do not leave valuables in the car.

KALALAU TRAIL

The **Kalalau Trail** ❿ starts here: 11 miles (18km) of gorgeous but strenuous trail snake along the Na Pali coastline, skirting isolated beaches and

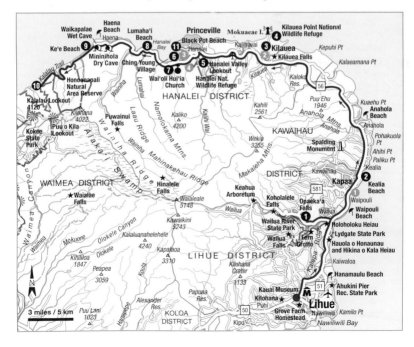

Hikers on the Kalalau Trail

ocean caves. The first two miles make a great day trip that includes coastal panoramas and takes you to the pristine Hanakapiai Valley, where a wide beach exists during the summer (in winter it's washed away by high surf). Swimming here is never recommended, but a picnic on the beach is. Even non-hikers should walk the first half-mile of the trail to the first lookout along the coast. It will make you want to come back someday and do the whole coast.

Finish your day back in Hanalei, following the same road back. Turn left just past Ching Young Village onto Ahi Street, then right at the stop sign onto Weke Road. Locals pronounce this 'vecky' road – the 'w' is tricky to pronounce in Hawaiian. Park at the beach part at the end of the road – right on the beach, if you wish, known as **Black Pot ⓫**. Then enjoy a sunset jump off the Hanalei Pier. Just do as the local kids do!

Food and Drink

① JAVA KAI

4-1384 Kuhio Highway; tel: 808-823 6887; www.javakaihawaii.com; daily 6am–7pm; $–$$

Java Kai Kapa'a is one of two Java Kais, the other is located in Hanalei. Coffee and baked goods are fresh, the bagels are as good as they get in Hawai'i, and the café serves as a social gathering place in both towns.

② KILAUEA BAKERY AND PAU HANA PIZZA

2484 Keneke Street; tel: 808-828 2020; www.kilaueabakery.com; daily 6am–9pm; $–$$

This place has something for everyone in the car – make your own pizza, where else is fresh fish an option? Or stop in for coffee and sticky buns in the morning.

③ THE HANALEI DOLPHIN

5-5016 Kuhio Highway; tel: 808-826 6113; www.hanaleidolphin.com; daily 11.30am–9pm; $$–$$$

This has been a local favorite for more than 40 years. As soon as you sit down, you'll understand why. The atmosphere is pure Hawai'i – green mountains, rolling river, kayakers paddling by and great food. Try the sushi or poke.

④ THE HANALEI GOURMET

5-5161 Kuhio Highway; tel: 808-826 2524; www.hanaleigourmet.com; daily 11am–9.30pm; $$

Once just a small deli without seats, the Hanalei Gourmet is now a full-fledged restaurant that prides itself on serving up healthy dishes – fresh local produce, dolphin-free tuna, low-sodium meats, fresh-baked bread and homemade dressing in a comfortable, casual atmosphere. Happy hour daily from 3.30–5.30pm.

Kauai Museum

LIHUE

An easy half-day tour of the county seat, complete with two plantation estates, Menehune handiwork, an easy kayak excursion and the Kauai Museum. Kitschy Hawaiiana and noodles, too.

DISTANCE: 6.5 miles (10km)
TIME: A half day
START: Kilohana
END: Grove Farm Homestead
POINTS TO NOTE: The tour is best done by car, as the town of Lihue is rather spread out. Children may get bored – the museums and estates have little to engage the young and active.

From Lihue town, head for **Kilohana** ❶, on Route 50 towards Poipu, one of several grand old Wilcox estates. Several of the rooms of this 1930s Tudor-style mansion have been restored, providing a sense of luxury as it was once lived on Kauai. Others now house galleries and boutiques. On the grounds you'll find **Gaylord's**, see ❶, one of the island's finest restaurants. To truly experience the old way of life, you can take a horse-drawn carriage ride around the estate, too.

Like nearly every other town on Kauai, Lihue started with sugar. It's now Kauai's largest community and its gov-

ernmental seat. It's not a tourist locus, but there are a couple of things to see, including the sugar mill that started it all and is still sometimes run to generate power. Take the highway back north to Lihue and turn right onto Rice Street. The **Kauai Museum** ❷ (www.kauai museum.org; Mon–Sat 10am–5pm) will be on your left. The museum packs lots of natural and cultural history into an hour visit, and offers day courses in *lauhala* weaving and *lei*-making. A gallery upstairs displays the work of local

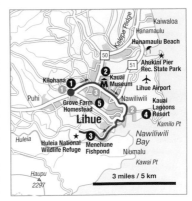

View from the Kauai Marriott

artists. Kauai is a laid-back, slow-paced island, so expect things to not always open on time. When in doubt, call ahead.

Food and Drink

❶ GAYLORD'S

3-2087 Kaumualii Highway; tel: 808-245 9593; www.gaylordskauai.com; Mon–Sat 11am–2.30pm and 5.30–8.30pm, Sun brunch 9am–1.30pm; $$$$

Gaylord's has top notch food – some would claim the best fine dining on Kauai. The atmosphere is fancier than other Kauai laid-back dining, but they won't turn you away for attire. Dinner reservations recommended.

❷ DUKE'S CANOE CLUB

Kauai Marriott Resort; tel: 808-256 9599; www.dukeskauai.com; daily from 11am; $$$

Duke's Canoe Club is exactly what you picture for a Hawai'i date night. There are too many kinds of fresh fish to pick from – but you won't go wrong no matter what you go with. The salad bar is extensive and the cocktails well done. Reservations recommended.

❸ HAMURA SAIMIN

2956 Kress Street; tel: 808-245 3271; daily 10am–10.30pm; $

This isn't just the best *saimin* on Kauai, it's the best in the state. Don't miss this Japanese-style comfort food – a noodle soup unlike anything you've had before.

THE WATERFRONT

Continue down Rice Street towards Nawiliwili, Kauai's picturesque commercial harbor. At the pier where the inter-island cruise ships dock, bear right past a huge, monolithic gray warehouse, which once stored sugar cane for shipment to the mainland, to Hulemalu Road. The road climbs to a lookout on the left. Below you is the Alakoko Fishpond, fed by the Hule'ia Stream descending from the Hoary Head Mountains beyond. Sometimes called the **Menehune Fishpond** ❸, legend says the Menehune people built this early example of aquafarming long before the Polynesians arrived. See it best, along with waterfalls and locations from Hollywood movies on a downstream river tour with Kauai Vacation Tours (www.kauaivacationtours.com).

Return to Nawiliwili and head for the **Kauai Lagoons Resort** ❹, home of the Kauai Marriott, the only place worth staying in Lihue. **Duke's Canoe Club**, see ❷ is one of Kauai's best hangouts. The local favorite, though, is back in town at **Hamura Saimin**, see ❸.

PLANTATION HOME

The **Grove Farm Homestead** ❺ (www.grovefarm.org; tours twice daily Mon, Wed and Thu; reservations required) is the former home of plantation founder George N. Wilcox. Located on Nawiliwili Road, this working homestead has original furnishings throughout.

Kayakers on the Wailua River

WAILUA

Around where the Wailua River meets the ocean, you will find a large number of important ancient Hawaiian sites. The royal Hawaiians held this area as sacred, and thus kapu to commoners. Come in the early morning or late afternoon to truly experience the culture behind the touristy lu'aus and leis.

DISTANCE: 25 miles (40km)
TIME: 2–3 hours
START: Lihue
END: Kapa'a
POINTS TO NOTE: Take a dive into this area on a day where you'd like to take it easy – this trip won't take long. Lydgate beach is the best spot on the island for young children, so pack the beach gear.

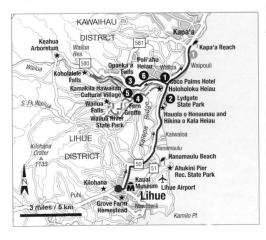

LEGENDARY KAUAI

Kauai legends and oral traditions are among Hawai'i's richest. In the last decade, visible remnants that embody ancient Hawaiian culture have become popular with travelers, including a gathering of rocks at Wailua. The site is a few hundred yards up Kuamo'o Road towards the mountains from the now defunct **Coco Palms Hotel ❶**, where Elvis once stayed and filmed *Blue Hawai'i*.

BIRTHSTONES AND WATERFALLS

Traveling north from Lihue on Highway 56, Kuhio Highway, turn right before crossing the Wailua River bridge at **Lydgate State Park ❷**, a favorite local beach with full facilities and a nice, protected swimming area perfect for young families. Walk

Opaeka'a Falls

towards the river. A grove of coconut palms shelters the **Hauola o Honaunaua** place of refuge for fugitives in old Hawai'i, and the Hikina o Kala Heiau. Take care not to move or change anything, nor leave any sign of your visit, as these sites are considered sacred.

Back in the car and just after the bridge, turn left onto Highway 580, Kuamo'o Road. Two miles (3km) up on the right is a parking lot for **Opaeka'a Falls** , most spectacular after heavy rains on Mount Wai'aleale. You can't see them, but shrimp lay eggs in the pool at the bottom of the 40ft (12-meter) waterfall. Do not try to reach the top of the falls, as water conditions change quickly and each year, tourists are lost to falls. Walk across the road for a broad view of the Wailua River gently snaking below, once lined with secret sacred temples all the way up to its origin on Waiale'ale; cliffs and bluffs along the way were *ali'i* burial places.

On the river, barge-like boats carry tourists to the **Fern Grotto** , where ferns grow profusely at the mouth of a lava tube. It's commercially promoted ad nauseam as a must-see but is actually somewhere you could pass by because of the intrusive showbiz style of the tour operator, both on the river and at the grotto. Better to spend your time and money visiting the streamside **Kamakila Hawaiian Village** at the junction of Kuamo'o and the highway, or renting a kayak and paddling up the river at your own pace. No forced serenades, no elbow-to-elbow crowds, just the beauty that is Kaua'i. Bring a picnic and take your time.

Continue to the end of Highway 580 for views of Mount Wai'aleale and to drive across the river. Park just after you cross the ford and walk downstream a bit to find a rope swing and swimming hole.

SACRIFICIAL SHRINES

Back on Highway 580, close to the main highway, there are several sacred outdoor shrines, including the **Poli'ahu Heiau** . Nearby is a bell stone, which long ago rang out when hit with a stone to announce royal births. Holoholoku Heiau, a sacrificial altar with royal birth-stones nearby, is an older heiau, and has more than coincidental resemblance to Tahitian temples. When you're done, skip the Smith's Luau, which is a bit hokey, and instead, delve into some Portuguese bean soup and pie at **Ono Family Restaurant**, see , (open for breakfast and lunch only) on Highway 56 before calling it a wrap.

Food and Drink

❶ ONO FAMILY RESTAURANT

4-1292 Kuhio Highway; tel: 808-822 1710; daily 7am to 2pm; $ – $$

This restaurant has the best macadamia nut pancakes in town. Portuguese bean soup is a local treat loved by all – hearty and thick, it's a meal unto itself.

'Iao Valley State Park

WEST MAUI AND LAHAINA

You can't help but notice the West Maui Mountains, an eroded and extinct volcano, now lusciously green. This tour takes you through, out and around the mountains to experience what makes Maui the world's first choice for a tropical vacation, from the Ia'o Needle to the endless beaches.

DISTANCE: 75 miles (120km)
TIME: A full day
START: Lahaina
END: Lahaina
POINTS TO NOTE: This itinerary centers on West Maui, starting and finishing in Lahaina. If staying in South Maui, you'll intercept the itinerary near Ma'alaea. Park the car when you get to Lahaina and plan to travel around on foot to truly see this little whaling town.

WEST MAUI MOUNTAINS

'Iao Valley – once the volcano's crater – is your first stop. Route 30 heads south out of Lahaina: passing beach parks with clear views across the Au'au Channel of Molokai, Lanai and Kaho'olawe, all part of Maui County. Between November and April, humpback whales (see page 11) nurture young in the sheltered waters. Signs point you to Wailuku, Maui's government seat nestled in the foothills above the more commercial Kahului. Continue on through both.

'IAO VALLEY STATE PARK

'Iao Valley State Park ❶ is the volcano's ancient crater at road's end and is idyllic, verdantly green and indubitably wet – 408ins (1,036cm) of rainfall yearly on the 5,788ft (1,764-meter) high Pu'u Kukui nearby; Lahaina, just 8 miles (13km) away by air, only gets 20ins (50cm). A stream skirts 'Iao Needle, the valley's 1,200ft (366-meter) -high focus, then descends to Wailuku. Follow the path around the park – it's a short, pleasant walk, even in a misty rain.

WAILUKU

Upon return to Wailuku, turn left onto Market Street, then to Vineyard Street. Several so-called antique shops are clustered here, filled mostly with dusty but wonderful old things and tantalizing Hawaiiana memorabilia. **Saeng's Thai Cuisine**, see ❶, on Vineyard lures travelers and locals alike. **Bailey House Museum ❷** is a museum of both traditional Hawaiian and missionary life.

Makena beach

SOUTH MAUI OPTION

Leaving Wailuku, consider a side trip to South Maui, especially **Wailea** ❸ and **Makena** ❹, with beaches and sunshine as good as, if not better, than Ka'anapali. Drive right through Kihei, an uninspired strip of condos and shopping centers. Wailea, however, is a luxury resort town with the extravagant Grand Wailea, the elegant Four Seasons, and the all-suites Kea Lani. For some sly humor, look at the Fernando Botero sculptures at the **Grand Wailea Resort** ❺.

WEST MAUI

Follow Routes 31 and 30 back to West Maui. Save Lahaina for last and head north to the **Kapalua Resort** town ❻, a development with superb golf courses, tennis courts, beaches and a deluxe mix of hotels and condominiums. Try **Sansei**, see ❷, at the Kapalua Shops for superb Japanese fare. Return towards Ka'anapali, developed as Hawai'i's first planned resort town nearly 60 years ago. Although overdeveloped for those seeking a quiet getaway, Ka'anapali draws some of Hawai'i's highest occupancies thanks to a mix of quality hotels, a 2-mile (3km) -long stretch of beach, shops, restaurants and a promenade that offers plenty of people watching.

Kapalua Resort golf course

Wo Hing Temple

WHALING CAPITAL

Don't miss **Whalers Village ❼**, home to two first-rate museums, one on whales and one on whaling. South of Ka'anapali, take the first turnoff for **Lahaina ❽**, the Pacific's whaling capital in the early 1800s. The main street is Front Street, paralleling the waterfront. The **Pioneer Inn** on Wharf Street and nearby banyan tree are good navigation references. The banyan tree was planted in 1873 and extends its canopy nearly an acre. The Pioneer Inn, built in 1901 for inter-island ferry passengers, has not-so-quiet rooms that are plain but economical. **Aina Nahu Lahaina**, a vacation condo on Wainee Street with Asian-inspired decor has waterfront views. Available almost everywhere is a brochure outlining a historical walking tour.

Two suggested stops are the **Wo Hing Temple** (858 Front Street; http://lahainarestoration.org/wo-hing-museum), built by a Chinese fraternal society in 1912 and now showing old Thomas Edison films of Hawai'i, and the **Baldwin House**, across from the Pioneer Inn. At the top end of Front Street is the **Lahaina Jodo Mission** (12 Ala Moana Street), where the largest Buddha outside of Asia ponders sunsets and yet more sunsets. If sunset approaches, drop anchor. Lahaina is one of the few places in Hawai'i with several pubs and restaurants right on the water – the best of which is **Lahaina Fish Co**., see ❸, because they catch their own.

Food and Drink

❶ SAENG'S THAI CUISINE
2119 W Vineyard Street, Wailuku; tel: 808-244 1567; Mon–Fri 11am–2.30pm and 5–9.30pm, Sat–Sun 5–9.30pm; $$
This Thai restaurant in Wailuku is an oasis in the midst of an urban area. The tasty menu is completely customizable, which makes it a great option for vegetarians.

❷ SANSEI
600 Office Road, Kapalua; tel: 808-669 6286; daily 5.15–10pm, Thu–Fri until 1am (over 21s only); $$$–$$$$
Sansei is one of the best dinner date and late hotspots on Maui. Reservations recommended. Always order one of the specials, and try the *panko ahi* roll. Late seating on Thursday and Friday involves karaoke – expect to hear some professionals!

❸ LAHAINA FISH CO.
831 Front Street, Lahaina; tel: 808-661 3472; www.lahainafishco.com; daily 11am–9.30pm; $$–$$$
This is the perfect place to try local fresh fish tacos. The *ahi poke* tacos are unlike any other fish taco you've tried. Perfect casual setting for an evening umbrella drink while watching the sun drop away.

Sunrise, Haleakala National Park

HALEAKALA AND UPCOUNTRY

Haleakala translates to the House of the Sun, and if you can get up early enough to witness sunrise at the summit, you'll feel you've truly seen the sun wake up. This tour takes you through many of Hawai'i's diverse ecosystems, and includes a trip to a lavender farm and a winery.

DISTANCE: 85 miles (137km) – out and back
TIME: A full day
START: Kahului Airport
END: Ho'okipa Beach
POINTS TO NOTE: Bring warm clothes; there's a huge difference in temperature between the beach and Haleakala's summit, and wear closed shoes – the hikes and ground at the top are made up of rough, ashy gravel. This tour is great for the whole family, no child will forget their first trip up a volcano. Catching sunrise requires a very early departure. Check the time it rises, then leave Kahului 1.5–2 hours before.

HALEAKALA

Haleakala is a dormant, which means very much not extinct, volcano – whose name literally means 'house of the sun.' Depending on what you did or didn't do last night, consider watching the Pacific's finest sunrise from the summit (10,023ft/3,040 meters). Allot two hours for the drive up from **Kahului Airport ❶**. On Route 36, there's a turnoff for the Haleakala Highway (Route 37) but only take it if you're chasing a summit sunrise.

Pa'ia

Instead, continue past the airport along Route 36 a few more miles to **Pa'ia ❷**, an old sugar town taken over by wind-surfers, new-age folks and their entourages. (From here, Route 36 continues to Hana, see page 84.) Be sure to stop here, as this town is full of hidden gems – shops, cafés and the occasional celebrity.

For breakfast, try savory crêpes at **Café des Amis**, see ❶, – the courtyard seating is the best, and the restaurant is wonderful with children.

Begin your ascent up the mountain via beautiful Baldwin Road. On your left is Mana Foods (49 Baldwin Avenue; www.manafoodsmaui.com), one of the oldest family-run natural foods stores in Hawai'i. Stop by to stock up on snacks to take to the summit.

Laidback Pa'ia *Above the clouds in Haleakala National Park*

UPCOUNTRY

Further along is **Makawao ❸**, a *paniolo* town settled by Portuguese immigrants working on area ranches. Its rough edges are softening with a scattering of new galleries, shops and eateries. Continue on, as you will come back through Makawao later. Follow the signs for Haleakala via Haleakala Highway. You're 'upcountry' now, on Haleakala's gentle slopes where the air is often brisk and the mood content. The road, after zigzagging through Makawao and Pukalani, twists like a crazed serpent all the way to Haleakala's top, taking about an hour more.

Haleakala National Park ❹ encompasses the 19-sq-mile (49-sq-km), 3,000ft (910-meter) -deep Haleakala Crater. The crater view is simply breathtaking. Contemplate the crater from two lookouts: **Kalahaku ❹** and **Pu'u Ula'ula ❺**, and then make your way to the summit. For avid hikers, consider Sliding Sands into the crater.

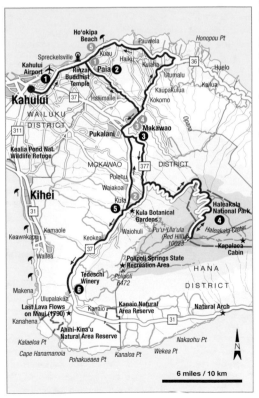

Barren bloom

Although it feels a bit like the moon, Haleakala is refuge for two unique species: the remarkable silver sword plant with its dagger-shaped silvery leaves and the once endangered Nene, or Hawaiian goose. Related to the sunflower, silver sword

Storefronts in Makawao

plants sometimes wait two decades or so before blooming just once. Growing up to a height of 8ft (2.5 meters), silver swords most commonly bloom in summer.

Kula

When you come back down, turn left onto Route 377 towards **Kula ❺**. The climate here is nearly perfect for the beautiful protea flower – you might stop at one of several protea farms in the area. **Kula Lodge**, see ❷, is good

for a late breakfast or, if you've spent all day, pizza for dinner. Follow Route 37 south as it narrows over idyllic countryside, more like Ireland than tropical Hawai'i. Alalakeiki Channel lies ahead; you can see Kahoolawe, Lanai, Molokai and a cute half moon islet called Molokini, a popular snorkeling spot.

Wine tasting

Along South Maui's coast, the resorts of Wailea look rather tiny from this 3,000ft (900-meter) elevation. Just past the rustic general store of Ulupalakua Ranch is the **Tedeschi Winery ❻**, the only commercial winery in Hawai'i, producing unique island brews like pineapple wine and Ulupalakua Red. After a few minutes in the tasting room, tour the winery and stretch your legs before heading back towards Kula. Stay left on Route 37 towards Pukalani. In Pukalani, turn right to Makawao for an hour or two of browsing or eating. Try **Polli's**, see ❸, for Mexican food, or **Casanova Italian Restaurant**, see ❹, which has a good takeout deli.

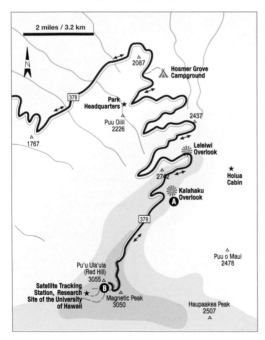

Windsurfers at Ho'okipa

Ho'okipa

Back along the same route to Pa'ia, turn right and follow Route 36 along the coast towards Kahului. A few minutes before Pa'ia, stop at Ho'okipa Beach, or view from a lookout on one of the bluffs. **Ho'okipa** is a world-class windsurfing spot because of ideal waves and wind. For an equally world-class dinner and drinks, try **Mama's Fish House**, see ⑤, just south of the beach.

Food and Drink

① CAFÉ DES AMIS

42 Baldwin Avenue, Paia; tel: 808-0579 6323; www.cdamaui.com; daily 8.30am–8.30pm; $$

Serves up Mediterranean and Indian food in a cute courtyard space in the heart of Pa'ia. Order the breakfast crêpes – any time of day. Happy hour every evening from 4–6pm.

② KULA LODGE

15200 Haleakala Highway, Kula; tel: 808-878 1535; www.kulalodge.com; daily 7am–9pm; $$–$$$

Perched on the side of Haleakala, Kula Lodge offers wonderful views and great brick-oven pizza. The interior is a mix – part cozy lodge, part hotel lobby-feel, and the service can be slow, however, the view makes it worth your time.

③ POLLI'S MEXICAN RESTAURANT MAUI

1202 Makawao Avenue, Makawao; tel: 808-572 7808; www.pollismexican restaurant.com; daily 11am–10pm; $$

Polli's is known for its Maui avocado guacamole. While Mexican fare in Hawai'i doesn't compare with that of California, this is as close as it gets. Casual atmosphere and good food.

④ CASANOVA ITALIAN RESTAURANT

1188 Makawao Avenue, Makawao, tel: 808-572 0220; www.casanovamaui.com; deli daily 7.30am–5.30pm, restaurant Mon–Tue and Thu–Sat 11.30am–2pm, Wed 5–9.30pm, with late night live music until 1am; $$–$$$

Perched at the top of Makawao town, this is the only fine dining and late night hangout in town. Some of the local folks dress up for dinner in the dining room, but you won't be turned away if you turn up in something more casual.

⑤ MAMA'S FISH HOUSE

799 Poho Place, Paia; tel: 808-579 8488; www.mamasfishhouse.com; daily 11am–10pm; $$$$

Mama's Fish House is the best place on Maui to enjoy fine dining with a view – and you'll pay a premium for it. The $16 Mai Tai is worth every cent, as is the fish curry with opah and ahi.

The road to Hana

HANA HIGHWAY

In spite of what the T-shirts say, there's nothing to 'survive' about the Hana Highway, except maybe sensory overload from the beauty of it all. This day trip takes you along the famous waterfall-lined Hana Highway to the town of Hana and Ohe'o Gulch with its refreshing pools.

DISTANCE: 110 miles (177km) round trip
TIME: A full day
START: Ho'kipa Beach
END: Pa'ia
POINTS TO NOTE: Not for those that get carsick – the road twists and turns and is slow, slow, slow. Be prepared to stop often – seeing the countless waterfalls, hidden neighborhoods, roadside fruit stands and more is part of the fun.

Built by convicts over half a century ago, the Hana Highway is a fine road, narrow but paved and well-marked. There are, however, many tight curves that make for slow travel – more than 600, by some counts. The road requires a full tank of gas. Traffic peaks late morning and is heavy again late afternoon.

The Hana Highway takes off on its own where the road changes from Route 36 to 360, at the junction with Route 400 beyond **Ho'okipa Beach ❶**. In Pa'ia, top up the gas tank and pick up a picnic lunch at **Mana Foods ❷** – one of the state's oldest and most loved grocers. Then

prepare to ooh and ah: the highway is a string of rich and lush forests, resplendent waterfalls at nearly every bend and fine ocean vistas. Pleasant rest stops, now or on the return, include **Waikamoi Ridge Trail Nature Walk ❸**, **Kaumahina State Park ❹** and **Ke'anae Arboretum ❺**. You'll find someone selling coconuts with a straw along the way – don't pass it up!

A must-stop, just before Hana, is **Wai'anapanapa State Park ❻**, with its black-sand beach and caves. Unattended 'honor stands' are the norm for fruit sales along the road – just leave your cash in the box.

Hana ❼ itself is a quaint little town with one general store, Hasegawa's (5165 Hana Highway). Rippling with quiet and unruffled serenity, there's hardly a touristy touch anywhere. The cross hovering over the town honors Paul Fagan, who built the hotel and started the ranch in the 1940s. **Travaasa Hana** (see page 97) is an expensive retreat favored by those who want privacy. Vacation rentals and a few B&Bs are also on hand, as well as rustic state cabins at Wai'anapanapa.

Bathing at Ohe'o Gulch

Ohe'o Gulch

Beyond Hana is the lower extent of Haleakala National Park. From mid-morning until late afternoon, you won't be alone at **Ohe'o Gulch** ❽, often called the Seven Sacred Pools and filled by a stream coming down Haleakala. Take the Waimoku Falls Trail to the upper pools for privacy. Towards sunset, the pools empty of people and they do indeed feel sacred.

At the pools' ocean outlet is a large grassy area ending abruptly on high cliffs. The stone remains of a fishing village are nearby. Dangerous currents make swimming a no-no here. For dinner head to the **Hana Ranch Restaurant**, see ❶. The real Hana Ranch, just past Hana town, is a welcoming sustainable farm and ranch selling a burgers and fresh fruit. Driving the road back at night is no problem.

Food and Drink

❶ HANA RANCH RESTAURANT

5031 Hana Highway, Hana; tel: 808-270 5280; daily L, D; $$–$$$

A killer burger and even better view. Sit outside under the patio.

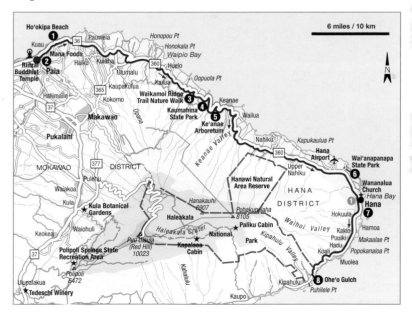

DIRECTORY

Hand-picked hotels and restaurants to suit all budgets and tastes, organized by area, plus select nightlife listings, an alphabetical listing of practical information, a language guide and an overview of the best books and films to give you a flavor of the city.

ACCOMMODATIONS

Resorts, hotels, inns, rental condominiums and bed-and-breakfasts abound in Hawai'i. The quality of accommodation varies widely, however. Many of the international luxury hotel chains (often at upward of $500 per night) have built brands around a certain standard of excellence. On the flipside, the quality of rooms at properties on the lower end of the scale can vary widely. Definitely do your research before you book.

Prices fluctuate considerably in Hawai'i; they are most commonly dictated by season and location. During the winter months, or rainy season, for instance, especially in resort areas such as Wailea on Maui, some high-end rooms might be $200–300 less than they are during high season. Location also determines price; the closer you are to a 'beachfront' location, the more expensive the nightly rate is likely to be. Most accommodations offer booking online via their websites and all of them take reservations by phone.

Bed-and-breakfast accommodations offer a more intimate overnight experience. Standards vary widely as they are regulated less than hotels, but most places offer a modicum of cleanliness and comfort. Hawai'i's Best Bed & Breakfasts (tel: 808-263 3100/toll free: 800-262 9912; www.bestbnb.com) has listings for B&Bs, boutique hotels and vacation rentals.

Vacation rentals are suitable for longer-term stays. They are a good option for families as most come with kitchenettes or full kitchens, enabling guests to prepare their own meals.

Price for a standard double room for one night without breakfast in high season:
$ = below $100
$$ = $100–200
$$$ = $201–300
$$$$ = above $300

Oahu

Aulani, a Disney Resort & Spa
92-1185 Aliinui Drive, Ko 'Olina, Kapolei, West Oahu; tel: 808-674 6200; http://resorts.disney.go.com/aulani-hawaii-resort; $$$$

Representing Disney's first hotel and timeshare development not connected to a theme park, this hotel mixes 'The Mouse' with tropical paradise to create a child-friendly atmosphere complete with roaming Disney characters in Hawaiian garb. An extensive pool complex includes a lazy river, a dive tank and two water slides. There's also an adults-only infinity pool.

Halekulani
2199 Kalia Road, Waikiki; tel: 808-923

2311; www.halekulani.com; $$$$

White is the theme at this elegant and chic resort; all of the rooms are robed in what the place calls its 'Seven Shades of White'. Private registration in your guest room adds to an exclusive feel. This hotel is Waikiki's finest, but there's not much for kids here.

Hilton Hawaiian Village Beach Resort and Spa

2005 Kalia Road, Waikiki; tel: 808-949 4321; www.hiltonhawaiianvillage.com; $$$

Five towers comprise what has become the largest hotel in Hawai'i, and a sixth is underway. The resort spans 22 acres (9 hectares) in all, including landscaped gardens, ponds and a pool complex that is great for kids. The resort even has its own pier (where the *Atlantis* submarine docks). All rooms have *lanais*.

Holiday Inn Waikiki Beachcomber Resort

2300 Kalakaua Avenue, Waikiki; tel: 808-922 4646; www.waikikibeachcomberresort.com; $$$

Centrally located in the heart of Waikiki. Once home of the legendary Don Ho show, the property now hosts a new stage show, dubbed the 'Magic of Polynesia'. All rooms have balconies; free Wi-Fi available on site.

Hyatt Regency Waikiki Resort and Spa

2424 Kalakaua Avenue, Waikiki; tel: 808-923 1234; www.hyattregencywaikiki.com; $$$

Centrally located just across the street from Kuhio Beach, this hotel has an unobstructed view of the Pacific. One highlight: the 10,000-sq-ft (900-sq-meter) Na Hoola spa, which boasts treatments including massages for soothing sore feet.

The Kahala Hotel

5000 Kahala Avenue, Kahala; tel: 808-739 8888; www.kahalaresort.com; $$$

A 10-minute drive east of Waikiki, this is Honolulu's poshest resort and is especially valued for its secluded oceanfront location. The dolphin lagoon is home to Atlantic bottlenose dolphins and tropical fish.

Moana Surfrider, a Westin Resort & Spa

2365 Kalakaua Avenue, Waikiki; tel: 808-922 3111; www.moana-surfrider.com; $$$$

Built in 1901, this Honolulu icon was Waikiki's first hotel and mixes nostalgic, early 20th-century ambiance and comfort from modern times. Enjoy tea-time on the veranda surrounding a huge banyan tree.

The Modern Honolulu

1775 Ala Moana Boulevard, Waikiki; tel: 808-943 5800; www.themodernhonolulu.com; $$$$

Arguably the trendiest hotel in town, the Modern is edgy and slick without being overbearingly so. Don't miss the pool complex, which includes an adults-only version of a wading pool, surrounded by 100 tons of sand.

The Royal Hawaiian

New Otani Kaimana Beach Hotel

2863 Kalakaua Avenue, Waikiki; tel: 808-923 1555; www.kaimana.com; $$$

Situated on the 'quiet end of Waikiki' (technically it's on Sans Souci Beach), this resort is one of the closest to Diamond Head and the Waikiki Aquarium. Oceanfront on Sans Souci Beach, known to locals as Kaimana Beach, at the foot of Diamond Head in Waikiki. Rooms are spacious but dated.

Outrigger Waikiki On The Beach

2335 Kalakaua Avenue, Waikiki; tel: 808-923 0711; www.outrigger.com; $$$

Located on the beach at Waikiki, this hotel is the best known of the family-run Outrigger Resorts on Oahu. Check out the good food and contemporary Hawaiian music at Duke's Canoe Club (see page 99).

Pacific Beach Hotel

2490 Kalakaua Avenue, Waikiki; tel: 808-923 4511/toll free: 800-367 6060; www.pacificbeachhotel.com; $$$

Located in Waikiki, across from the beach, this hotel comprises two towers; every room has a *lanai*. The centerpiece of the property is a spectacular 3-story, 280,000-gallon indoor oceanarium tank, visible from the hotel's three restaurants.

The Royal Hawaiian, a Luxury Collection Resort

2259 Kalakaua Avenue, Waikiki; tel: 808-923 7311; www.royal-hawaiian.com; $$$$

With its coral-pink stucco and Moorish-Spanish design, the 'Pink Palace of the Pacific' is a landmark on Waikiki Beach. The hotel sits smack in the middle of Waikiki's shopping area.

Trump International Hotel Waikiki Beach Walk

223 Saratoga Road, Waikiki; tel: 808-683 7777; www.trumphotelcollection.com/waikiki; $$$$

Chic, modern, and sophisticated, this property boasts apartment-style living, complete with mini-kitchens and luxurious bathrooms. A beach concierge sets up guests with bags and umbrellas for the beach across the street.

Turtle Bay Resort

57-091 Kamehameha Highway, Kahuku, North Shore; tel: 808-293 6000; www.turtlebayresort.com; $$$

Perched on the edge of Kuilima Point, Turtle Bay is the North Shore's only resort. Guest rooms average 500 sq ft (51 sq meters), and children will love the 80ft (23-meter) water slide. The resort's best claim to fame? It has appeared in countless television shows and films, most famously *Lost* and *Forgetting Sarah Marshall*.

Hawai'i Island

Fairmont Orchid Hawai'i

One North Kaniku Drive, Kohala Coast; tel: 808-885 2000; www.fairmont.com/orchid; $$$$

A peaceful lagoon and beach popular with sunning sea turtles are among the attractions at this sprawling luxury resort. While standard accommodations are fine for most travelers, concierge-level rooms, which include access to all-day snacks, are exquisite. Rental bikes available.

Four Seasons Resort Hualalai

72-100 Kaupulehu Drive, Kona; tel: 808-325 8000; www.fourseasons.com/hualalai; $$$$
Everything at this resort revolves around bungalows, 36 of which are house rooms and suites. This means everything at the resort is spread out, adding to a feeling of calm and privacy. Informative exhibits are on view at the resort's Hawaiian Interpretive Center. Be sure to play the PGA-standard golf course.

Hapuna Beach Prince Hotel

62-100 Kauna'oa Drive, Kohala Coast; tel: 808-880 1111; www.hapunabeachprince hotel.com; $$$
This hotel sits on one of the largest sand beaches on Hawai'i Island, and all rooms face the ocean. The pool overlooks the beach as well. Large rooms boast marble bathrooms and private *lanais*. The on-site golf course, designed by Arnold Palmer, is a favorite among locals.

Hilo Naniloa Hotel

93 Banyan Drive, Hilo; tel: 808-969 3333; www.aquaresorts.com/hotels/hilo-naniloa-hotel; $$

Two towers comprise this hotel, which looks out over Hilo Bay. Rooms come standard with *lanais* and sofa beds; those in the Mauna Kea tower also include complimentary high-speed internet access. The hotel is dated, but clean.

Hilton Waikoloa Village

69-425 Waikoloa Beach Drive, Waikoloa; tel: 808-886 1234; www.hiltonwaikoloavillage. com; $$$
Yes, there actually are dolphins in the lagoon at this 62-acre (25-hectare) mega-resort, and you can pay to swim with them. There also are water slides, a nightly torch-lighting ceremony and a cornucopia of restaurant options. If you dislike crowds, or want to be able to quickly 'run up to the room,' this very large resort may not be for you.

Holualoa Inn

76-5932 Mamalahoa Highway, Holualoa; tel: 808-324 1121; www.holualoainn.com; $$$
This Kona area inn is located in a cedar home on a 30-acre (12-hectare) coffee-country estate, a few miles above Kona. Rooms boast an Asian theme, and daily breakfasts comprise coffee with fruits, vegetables and eggs harvested on site.

Kilauea Lodge

19-3948 Old Volcano Road, Volcano; tel: 808-967 7366; www.kilaualodge.com; $$$
One mile (1.6km) from the entrance of Hawai'i Volcanoes National Park, this

lodge was built as a YMCA camp in the 1930s. Today, rooms feature antiques, rich quilts and Hawaiian artwork. Some even boast fireplaces. Off-site cottages also are available.

King Kamehameha's Kona Beach Hotel

75-5660 Palani Road, Kona; tel: 808-329 2911; www.konabeachhotel.com; $$

Rooms at this landmark hotel are modern and include sliding plantation shutter screens. The hotel also has a fitness center and spa. It is an easy walk to downtown Kona attractions.

Manago Hotel

82-6151 Mamalahoa Highway, Captain Cook; tel: 808-323 2642; www.manago hotel.com; $

This family-run hotel in the center of Captain Cook overlooks Kealakekua Bay. About two thirds of the hotel's rooms have private bathrooms; the rest share bathrooms. The hotel also boasts a Japanese room with tatami mats and a futon.

Mauna Lani Bay Hotel & Bungalows

68-1400 Mauna Lani Drive, Kohala Coast; tel: 808-885 6622; www.maunalani.com; $$$

Guests to this classic Hawai'i Island resort are greeted by an open-air lobby with cathedral ceilings, and the breathtaking architecture continues in the spacious-yet-understated guest rooms.

Free cultural and educational programs provide guests with unqiue local knowledge.

Palms Cliff House

28-3514 Mamalahoa Highway, Honomu; tel: 808-963 6076; www.palmscliffhouse. com; $$$

This luxurious B&B on the bluffs overlooking the Pacific has been voted best in the East Side consistently since it was built in 2000. Rooms and suites boast tropical decor, while the communal areas offer a number of cozy nooks perfect for snuggling in and reading books.

Puakea Ranch

56-2864 Akoni Pule Highway, Hawi; tel: 808-315 0805; www.puakearanch.com; $$$$

Guests of this historic country estate enjoy their own private swimming pools, horseback riding, and plenty of fresh fruit and veggies to pick whenever they wish. The ranch is 10 minutes to the closest beach and about 15 minutes outside Hawi Town. Staying here is a true escape.

Volcano House

Crater Rim Drive, Hawai'i Volcanoes National Park; tel: 808-441 7750; www.hawaiivolcanohouse.com; $$

Valued for its location inside the Hawai'i Volcanoes National Park overlooking Halema'uma'u crater, this hotel reopened in 2013 after years of renovation. On certain nights, guests can see

the glow of molten lava from the hotel's main lanai.

Molokai

Hotel Molokai

1300 Kamehameha V Highway, Kaunakakai; tel: 808-660 3408; www.hotelmolokai.com; $$

A-frame buildings and other low-lying buildings are de rigueur at this property, arguably the biggest and most notable hotel in Kaunakakai. Rooms are basic with a Polynesian decor; they all look out on a central lawn.

Lanai

Four Seasons Resort Lanai, The Lodge at Koʻele

One Keomoku Highway, Lanai City; tel: 808-565 4000; www.fourseasons.com/koele; $$$$

This resort doesn't feel Hawaiian; it is a cool mountain retreat in the uplands of Lanai. Still, it is luxurious. Rooms are outfitted with thick, comfy furniture, as well as spacious bathrooms. Outside, activities include everything from horseback riding to tennis, golf and clay-shooting.

Four Seasons Resort Lanai, at Manele Bay

One Manele Bay Road, Lanai City; tel: 808-565 2000; www.fourseasons.com/manelebay; $$$$

Set on a cliff overlooking the beach at pristine Hulopoʻe Bay, this swanky property is owned by Larry Ellison, who also owns the island. Rooms offer modern conveniences with a traditional Hawaiian spin; private *lanais* boast wicker furniture and plenty of space to move around. The resort also borders a marine preserve, where there is great snorkeling and stellar hiking.

Hotel Lanai

828 Lanai Avenue, Lanai City; tel: 808-565 7211; www.hotellanai.com; $$$

This cozy little inn, which dates to 1923, is the affordable way to visit Lanai, especially considering that the other two properties on island are Four Seasons. Rooms are modest and feature antique furniture and hand-sewn Hawaiian quilts. Don't forget to try the Lanai City Grill, one of the best restaurants in town.

Kauai

Courtyard Kauai at Coconut Beach

650 Aleka Loop, Kapaa; tel: 808-822 3455; www.marriott.com/hotels/travel/lihku-courtyard-kauai-at-coconut-beach; $$

The Courtyard Kauaʻi at Coconut Beach is tucked away from the others, on a nice stretch of beach. Spacious rooms have free Wi-Fi, and all have private *lanais*. The rooms are standard, no bells and whistles, but the resort is conveniently located for sightseeing and the fire pits and hammocks lining the beach are lovely in the afternoons.

Garden Island Inn

3445 Wilcox Road, Lihuʻe; tel: 808-245 7227; www.gardenislandinn.com; $$

The Presidential Suite at the St. Regis Princeville Resort

Budget-conscious travelers love this three-story hotel across the street from Kalapaki Beach and adjacent to the Marriott (and all of its restaurants). The property is a short walk from the Anchor Cove shopping center and Duke's Bar.

Grand Hyatt Kauai Resort and Spa

1571 Po'ipu Road, Koloa; tel: 808-742 1234; www.grandhyattkauai.com; $$$$

If a mega-resort can be understated, this property proves the point. The hotel is cut into the cliffs overlooking an undeveloped coastline, providing stellar views. Most of the rooms have ocean views. The pool area boasts both freshwater and saltwater swimming lagoons and are the best pools for children on the island.

Hanalei Bay Resort

5380 Honoiki Road, Princeville; tel: 808-826 6522; www.hanaleibayresort.com; $$$

Vistas are everything at this resort; guests are hard-pressed to avoid views of Hanalei. Rooms are casual and fun, featuring rattan furniture and island art. The upper-level pool has lava-rock waterfalls and a child-friendly sand beach. Largely timeshare, but some rooms available.

Hanalei Colony Resort

5-7130 Kuhio Highway, Haena; tel: 808-826 6235; www.hcr.com; $$$

The only true beachfront resort on the North Shore, this 5-acre (2-hectare) property is great for its simplicity. There are no phones, TVs or stereos, but the place does offer Wi-Fi. There's also an art gallery, spa and restaurant on site.

Kauai Marriott Resort on Kalapaki Beach

3610 Rice Street, Lihu'e; tel: 808-245 5050; www.kauaimarriott.com; $$$

Everything is big at this beachfront resort, from the 26,000-sq-ft (2,400-sq-meter) swimming pool to the tropical garden, spacious guest rooms, and the view of the Haupu Ridge. Originally the Westin Kauai, a Hemmetter resort, it's been remodeled but maintains its original grandeur. The resort sits about a mile from Kauai International Airport, and a free shuttle is available.

Koa Kea Hotel and Resort

2251 Po'ipu Road, Koloa; tel: 808-828 8888; www.koakea.com; $$$$

Families are not welcome at this über-luxurious resort, which mixes contemporary Asian touches with white, blue and sandy tones. On account of its limited clientele and small size, it has a calmer vibe than many of the bigger resorts in the area. You'll feel further off the beaten path than anywhere else on island.

St. Regis Princeville Resort

5520 Ka Huku Road, Princeville; tel: 808-826 9644; www.princevillehotelhawaii.com; $$$$

Little touches make a huge difference in the rooms at this North Shore gem. Among them: lighted closets, original artwork and marble bathrooms with pri-

The pool at the Sheraton Kauai Resort

vacy windows. The hotel is so swanky, so upscale, that it almost sticks out from the serene landscape of Hanalei Bay. With everything available within the resort and stunning views, you can spend your entire vacation on-site.

Sheraton Kauai Resort

2440 Ho'onani Road, Koloa; tel: 808-742 1661; www.sheraton-kauai.com; $$$$

Oceanfront takes on new meaning at this resort, where crashing waves actually splash guests in the ocean wing. Elsewhere on property, three fire pits provide great places for visitors to interact. The hotel is a short walk to restaurants in Po'ipu, large and spread out, and family-friendly.

Waimea Plantation Cottages

9400 Kaumuali'i Highway, Waimea; tel: 808-338 1625; www.waimeaplantation. com; $$$

The homes of different sizes on this historic plot mix porches and plantation-era furnishings with modern kitchens and cable TV. The property also offers hammocks, a spa and a museum. Located on one of the island's black-sand beaches.

Best Western Pioneer Inn

658 Wharf Street, Lahaina; tel: 808-661 3636; www.pioneerinnmaui.com; $$

Built in 1901, this historic hotel looks out on the bustling harbor and sits next to the city's famous banyan tree. Rooms sport decor to match the building's cen-

tury-old roots. If you need quiet, ask for a room facing the courtyard.

Fairmont Kea Lani Maui

4100 Wailea Alanui Drive, Wailea; tel: 808-875 4100; www.fairmont.com/kealani; $$$$

With white spires and tiled archways, this resort looks like something out of Morocco. All rooms are suites and 37 of them are two-story villas. The beach is family-friendly and gorgeous, and the hotel is walking distance to the Shops at Wailea retail complex. A host of family-ly-friendly programs are available year-round. Ko, the on-site restaurant, serves authentic Hawaiian cuisine.

Four Seasons Resort Maui at Wailea

3900 Wailea Alanui Drive, Wailea; tel: 808-874 8000; www.fourseasons.com/maui; $$$$

Elegant furnishings, fresh flowers and sumptuous bed linens characterize rooms at this iconic Four Seaons on Wailea Beach. On-site restaurants include Wolfgang Puck's Spago and DUO Steak & Seafood. Pool services include Evian spritzers and hand-passed freshly cut fruit. Home to the Maui Film Festival each summer, but you'll find a celebrity or two year-round.

Grand Wailea Resort Hotel & Spa

3850 Wailea Alanui Drive, Wailea; tel: 808-875 1234; www.grandwailea.com; $$$$

You've never seen a pool like the one at this 40-acre (16-hectare) resort; it fea-

tures a 'canyon riverpool,' slides, caves, a Tarzan swing and a water elevator. The water theme continues inside Spa Grande, which offers one of the most comprehensive hydrotherapy programs on the island. The resort is a family's delight, with programs for children and a separate, quiet adult pool as well.

Hotel Wailea

555 Kaukahi Street, Wailea; tel: 808-874 0500; www.hotelwailea.com; $$$$

Set back from the beaches of Wailea, this resort is a true luxury – in fact, it's the nicest off-beach resort in all of Maui. All of the rooms are suites that include comfortable furniture, private *lanais* and deep soaking tubs. The on-site spa specializes in facials.

Hyatt Regency Maui Resort and Spa

200 Nohea Kai Drive, Ka'anapali; tel: 808-661 1234; www.maui.hyatt.com; $$$$

Water features, museum-quality art and penguins welcome guests to this bustling resort at the southern end of Ka'anapali Beach. The property has become known for its spa, Spa Moana, and its *lu'au*, the spectacular 'Drums of the Pacific' show that draws visitors from all over the island.

Ka'anapali Beach Hotel

2525 Ka'anapali Parkway, Ka'anapali; tel: 808-661 0011; www.kbhmaui.com; $$$

The least upscale of Ka'anapali's hotels is also its most storied; KBH has been welcoming guests for almost 50 years. The staff are well-versed in local knowledge they can share with guests one-on-one or during classes throughout the week. Rooms are decorated in Hawaiiana style – kitschy but fun.

Lahaina Inn

127 Lahainaluna Road, Lahaina; tel: 808-661 0577; www.lahainainn.com; $$$

This restored 1860s boutique hotel is located off Front Street in Lahaina, putting it right in the center of all of the town's action. Rooms feature antique furnishings and all guests receive breakfast every day. No children under 15 years.

Makena Beach & Golf Resort

5400 Makena Alanui, Makena; tel: 808-874 1111; www.makenaresortmaui.com; $$$

Located near Makena Beach, south of Wailea, this resort (formerly known as the Maui Prince) offers scenic views of neighboring islands and access to Maui's most popular public beach. The most remote of the hotels along the coast, it truly feels quiet and private. The hotel also offers on-site tennis courts, as well as activities such as diving and snorkeling.

The Mauian

5441 Lower Honoapi'ilani Road, Napili; tel: 808-669 6205; www.mauian.com; $$

This charming, beachfront hideaway is set right on one of West Maui's finest beaches. Rooms are outfitted with 'island' decor and come standard with

private *lanais*. All guests also receive complimentary Continental breakfast every day.

Paia Inn

93 Hana Highway, Paia; tel: 808-579 6000; www.paiainn.com; $$

Originally built as a boarding house in 1927, this property has since been converted into a modest inn. Rooms are surprisingly modern and come with an iPod clock/radio and a fully stocked minibar. One word of warning: there is no elevator.

The Ritz-Carlton, Kapalua

One Ritz-Carlton Drive, Kapalua; tel: 808-669 6200; www.ritzcarlton.com; $$$$

The culture of Maui is alive and well at this resort, which employs a cultural specialist to inform guests about local history. Grown-ups love the pool and hot tubs that are open 24 hours; kids love the on-site Environmental Education Center. The property doesn't have a beach of its own, but it is a short walk to D.T. Fleming Beach, one of the island's best.

Royal Lahaina Resort

2780 Keka'a Drive, Ka'anapali; tel: 808-661 3611; www.royallahaina.com; $$$$

Dating back to 1962, when it debuted as Ka'anapali's first hotel, this property remains the Grand Dame of the resort stretch. Rooms are decorated with dark teak furnishings. For a taste of yesteryear, hit the Don the Beachcomber bar, which is reputed to be the home of the Mai Tai.

Sheraton Maui Resort & Spa

2605 Ka'anapali Parkway, Ka'anapali; tel: 808-661 0031; www.sheraton-maui.com; $$$$

This white resort sits next to and on top of the 80ft (23-meter) -high Puu Keka'a, also known as Black Rock, from which divers leap in a nightly torch-lighting and cliff-diving ritual. Rooms are spacious with modern touches such as stereo systems. There's also great snorkeling right off the beach.

Travaasa Hana

5031 Hana Highway, Hana; tel: 888-820 1043; www.travaasa.com/hana; $$$$

Casual elegance is perfected at this intimate and upscale resort in Maui's most remote town. The property comprises two adjacent sites; one where families are welcome, and another for adults only. All guests have access to a multitude of activities each day. Both the spa and on-site restaurant are stellar.

The Westin Maui Resort & Spa

2365 Ka'anapali Parkway, Ka'anapali; tel: 808-667 2525; www.westinmaui.com; $$$$

Waterfalls and lagoons connect the two towers of this resort, which is great for families. All rooms boast Westin's signature Heavenly Bed, and also contain a sofa bed. The Wailele Polynesian Lu'au includes Maui's only fireknife dance. There's also a free shuttle to Lahaina, where parking can be difficult.

Saimin (Japanese noodle soup)

RESTAURANTS

Hawai'i has truly become a foodie's delight. With a multitude of good restaurants serving up a bevy of different cuisines, there are options for all price ranges. The chefs here enjoy experimenting, adding a little Asian to Continental, or Italian to Pacific. And all use Hawai'i-grown ingredients whenever possible. 'Pacific Rim' cuisine has gained international respect and because Hawai'i is a melting pot of cultures, there are numerous ethnic cuisines to be enjoyed, too: Thai, Vietnamese, Korean, Chinese and Japanese are only a few of the ones you see every day.

If you're eating breakfast or lunch, reservations aren't really necessary. For dinner, however, especially in some of the busier tourist spots such as Honolulu on Oahu and Lahaina or Paia on Maui, it's always a good idea to book a table in advance by phone or online.

Etiquette in Hawaiian restaurants is the same as it is in the rest of the US. Beach attire is generally acceptable for breakfast and lunch, but for dinner

> Price categories are for a two-course meal, paired with a glass of wine, if served at the restaurant.
> $ = less than $25
> $$ = $25–50
> $$$ = $50–75
> $$$$ = $75 and up

guests should spruce up a bit (i.e. no ball caps or tank tops). Tipping servers also is customary; 15 percent is standard for average service, while good service deserves 20 percent.

Oahu

Honolulu
Alan Wong's Restaurant
1857 S. King Street; tel: 808-949 2526; www.alanwongs.com; $$$$
Chef Wong made a name for himself by taking creative and innovative approaches to traditional Island cuisine, and that's exactly what he continues to do at this restaurant, one of the best in all of Hawai'i. Fans rave about the 'Da Bag,' which comprises clams and *kalua* pig steamed in an aluminium pouch. Reservations essential.

Arancino
255 Beach Walk; tel: 808-923 5557; www.arancino.com; $$$
This is the first of four locations for the popular local Italian chain, and it's still the best. Pasta dishes such as black tiger shrimp and arugula in homemade tomato sauce are executed to perfection. Homemade desserts such as cannolis don't disappoint either.

BLT Steak
Trump Hotel Waikiki, 223 Saratoga Road;

www.trumphotelcollection.com/waikiki; tel: 808-683 7777; $$$$
This French spin on an American steakhouse offers prime cuts of beef, fresh seafood and a variety of side dishes. There's also a raw bar – one of the best in town. Because the Trump attracts celebrities, you might even find yourself dining with the stars.

Chef Mavro
1969 S. King Street; tel: 808-944 4714; www.chefmavro.com; $$$$
Some see chef George Mavrothalassitis as a bit eccentric; he has been known to spend hundreds of dollars tracking down the freshest fish for certain dishes. The result is a French-inspired menu like none other, complete with wine pairings. Menu changes quarterly. Reservations essential.

Cholo's
62-250 Kamehameha Highway, Hale'iwa; tel: 808-637 3059; $$
This homestyle Mexican restaurant is located in the North Shore Marketplace. The highlights are fish tacos and margaritas in giant goblets the size of small fish tanks. The place boasts authentic, colorful artwork from Mexico; most of it is for sale.

Duke's Canoe Club
Outrigger Waikiki Hotel, 2335 Kalakaua Avenue; tel: 808-922 2268; www.dukes waikiki.com; $$
Memorabilia on the walls of this oceanfront restaurant pays tribute to Duke Hakanamoku, the father of modern surfing. The food is pretty appealing, too; the place is known for its tasty prime rib and rotisserie chicken. Sunday brunch here is good value.

Hau Tree Lanai
New Otani Kaimana Beach Hotel, 2863 Kalakaua Avenue; tel: 808-921 7066; www.kaimana.com; $$
Follow in the footsteps of author Robert Louis Stevenson as you sit under the *hau* tree at this beachside seafood restaurant. Kids will love the purple *poi* pancakes at breakfast. Breakfast and lunch only.

Kona Brewing Company
Koko Marina Shopping Center, 7192 Kalanianaole Highway; tel: 808-396 5662; $$
This popular local hangout has 24 local brews on tap and sits perched on Koko Marina in Hawai'i Kai. All that beer should be accompanied by nachos – order the kalua pig version for smoky, moist meat.

Little Village Noodle House
1113 Smith Street; tel: 808-545 3008; www.littlevillagehawaii.com; $
Smack in the heart of Honolulu's Chinatown, this restaurant serves up an eclectic, pan-Chinese menu. In particular, vegetarian options abound; the

dried green beans are addictive. Public-paid parking available next door.

Lucky Belly

50 N. Hotel Street; tel: 808-531 1888; www.luckybelly.com; $$

Pork lovers will adore this Modernist and upscale eatery, which elevates the swine to gastronomic heaven. Try the pork belly *bao* to start, then move on to *ramen* with pork belly, bacon and sausage. Meat-free salads also available.

Michel's at the Colony Surf

Colony Surf, 2895 Kalakaua Avenue; tel: 808-923 6552; www.michelshawaii.com; $$$$

Lovers, this is the place for you. Restaurant windows sit mere inches from the ocean. An exquisite French menu includes traditional options such as escargot and foie gras, as well as newer items that incorporate local seafood. Dinner only. Reservations essential.

The Modern

1775 Ala Moana Boulevard; tel: 808-943 5900; www.morimotowaikiki.com; $$$$

Try the *kim chee* tofu dish made tableside at this upscale eatery from TV Iron Chef Morimoto. The restaurant serves mostly super-fresh sushi and sashimi – largely caught in local waters the day you dine.

MW Restaurant

1528 Kapiolani Boulevard; tel: 808-955 6505; www.mwrestaurant.com; $$$

The brains behind this popular local restaurant are Wade Ueoka and Michelle Karr-Ueoka, a husband-and-wife team from Alan Wong's, who strive to blend local seafood and produce. Try the hearty oxtail soup. Reservations recommended.

Rainbow Drive-In

3308 Kana'ina Avenue; tel: 808-737 0177; www.rainbowdrivein.com; $

Food at this drive-in restaurant is about as authentic as Hawaiian food can get. The signature dish is the Plate Lunch, with two scoops of rice, one scoop of macaroni salad and your choice of protein. Daily specials – particularly the beef stew – are worth sampling, too. Breakfasts here are also delicious.

Roy's Waikiki Beach

226 Lewers Street; tel: 808-923 7697; www.roysrestaurant.com; $$$$

This isn't Roy Yamaguchi's first restaurant in Honolulu, but it is by far the most popular. Located in the Beach Walk development, the eatery turns out Roy's signature spin on Island cuisine, blending European techniques and Asian cuisine.

Sorabol

805 Ke'eaumoku Street; tel: 808-947 3113; www.sorabolhawaii.com; $$

This 24-hour eatery represents the largest Korean restaurant in the city, and is a favorite spot among late-

A beachside table at Beach Tree

night revelers. Traditional dishes such as *bi bim bap* and *kal bi* are above average.

Ted's Bakery

59-024 Kamehameha Highway, Sunset Beach; tel: 808-638 597; www.tedsbakery. com; $

There's more to this North Shore hole-in-the-wall than chocolate cream pies; Ted's is a classic sandwich shop as well, serving up giant submarine sandwiches, mixed plate lunches and more. Buy an extra roll or two, sit outside and feed the local chickens.

Teddy's Bigger Burgers

134 Kapahulu Avenue; tel: 808-926 3444; www.teddysbiggerburgers.com; $

Hawaiians love their comfort food, and the burgers (and shakes and fries) at Teddy's rank among the best. There are other locations around town but this is the original. It even has a place to store surfboards for customers who come in off the beach.

Vintage Cave

1450 Ala Moana Boulevard; tel: 808-441 1744; www.vintagecave.com; $$$$

Small portions and Japanese sensibility characterize the experience at this sophisticated eatery, which serves a set menu every night. Attire here is semi-formal for men and women alike. Reservations essential. Consider making reservations a month in advance.

Wai'oli Tea Room

2950 Manoa Road; tel: 808-988 5800; $$

Experiencing old-fashioned 'high tea' at this tearoom in the hills above Honolulu feels like stepping into someone's house, though it is run by the Salvation Army and profits go towards a local rehabilitation center. Tea is hot, goodies are fresh and delicious, and photos and clippings on the walls are like a walk down memory lane.

Hawai'i Island

Beach Tree at the Four Seasons Resort Hualalai

Four Seasons Resort Hualalai; 72-100 Ka'upulehu Drive, Kailua-Kona; tel: 808-325 8000; www.fourseasons.com/ hualalai/dining/restaurants/beach_tree; $$$

Waves break just beyond your table at this alfresco, modern eatery that combines cuisine from Italy and Spain. Though the atmosphere feels a bit formal, the restaurant actually is great for kids, with chalk and chalkboards for every table.

Bite Me Fish Market Bar & Grill

425 Kealakehe Parkway; tel: 808-327 3474; www.bitemefishmarket.com; $

You can't get fish much fresher than what's on offer here; the joint looks out on the boat ramp at the Bite Me Fish Market in Honokohau Harbor. Sandwiches are named after fishing lures. Try the fish tacos for a real treat.

Sophisticated cuisine at Brown's Beach House

Brown's Beach House at the Fairmont Orchid Hawai'i

1 North Kaniku Drive, Kohala Coast; tel: 808-885 2000; www.fairmont.com/orchid; $$$

Every restaurant on Hawai'i Island serves local seafood, but few do it as expertly as Brown's. Consider the Keahole lobster tails cooked with lilikoi Hawaiian vanilla bean gastrique. Other dishes incorporate daikon, ginger, lavender and different local ingredients.

The Coffee Shack

83-5799 Mamalahoa Highway, Captain Cook; tel: 808-328 9555; www.coffee shack.com; $

Think of this diner as a Hawaiian spin on a traditional Greasy Spoon; it's only open for lunch and dinner, but breakfasts are huge and all of the breads are homemade. Beans for the house coffee are grown on the mountainside directly below the lanai.

Huggo's

75-5828 Kahakai Road; tel: 808-329 1493; www.huggos.com; $$$

There aren't many fancy restaurants in Kailua, but this oceanfront eatery is the fanciest (and most expensive) of the bunch. Local seafood is the specialty here; also, try the guava-braised baby back ribs.

Kawaihae Seafood Bar & Grill

61-3642 Kawaihae Harbor, Kawaihae; tel: 808-880 9393; www.seafood barandgrill.com; $$

The building that houses this restaurant dates back to the 1850s. If you're with a big group, order off the *pupu* (appetizer) menu; if you like vegetables, the Island Salad comprises the very best of the island's produce of the day.

Kona Brewing Company Pub and Brewery

75-5629 Kuakini Highway; tel: 808-329 2739; www.konabrewingco.com; $$

Every visitor to Kailua-Kona should come here and dine on the patio at least once. Never mind that the place is in an industrial part of town; the microbrews are stupendous and the Polynesian-themed menu (think pulled-pork quesadillas) is great for any occasion.

Merriman's

65-1227 Opelo Road, Waimea; tel: 808-885 6822; www.merrimanshawaii.com; $$$–$$$$

Renowned Hawaiian chef Peter Merriman considers this his signature restaurant, which means the food is fresh, exciting and delicious. Try the seared ahi or any of the braised meats, all of which are raised locally to the restaurant's specifications. Reservations essential.

The Seaside Restaurant & Aqua Farm

1790 Kalaniana'ole Avenue, Hilo;

tel: 808-935 8825; $$

Sure, the food here is tasty (try the fried *aholehole*), but the real attraction is the 30-acre (12-hectare) brackish-water fishpond outside, where the Nakagawa family raise their own fish. Reservations suggested.

Sushi Rock

55-3435 Akone Pule Highway, Hawi; tel: 808-889 5900; www.sushirockrestaurant. net; $$

There's no question that this small and quirky eatery serves up some of the best sushi on the entire island. Rolls change daily and often incorporate local ingredients with a twist – beef, lamb, or another type of meat. There's also a full bar (and a lengthy cocktail list).

Village Burger

67-1185 Mamalahoa Highway, Waimea; tel: 808-885 7319; www.villageburgerwaimea. com; $

Burgers from this Parker Ranch Center eatery aren't just any old hamburgers; they're locally raised, grass-fed, hormone-free hamburgers. Toppings include locally produced bacon, avocadoes and cheese. Even the ice cream for the house shakes is made in town.

Molokai

Molokai Pizza Café

15 Kaunakakai Place, Kaunakakai; tel: 808-553 3288; $–$$

In addition to serving pizza (as the name suggests), this restaurant offers a mean prime rib and surprisingly good Mexican food. The atmosphere is casual and fun; at times, even on sparsely populated Molokai, it can actually feel lively.

Lanai

Dining Room

Four Seasons Resort Lanai, The Lodge at Ko'ele, 1 Keomoku Highway; tel: 808-565 4580; www.fourseasons.com/koele; $$$

The menu at this upscale in-lobby restaurant features a Hawaiian spin on the nature-to-table concept, incorporating as many locally grown and harvested items as possible (including meat). The multi-course chef's tasting menu with wine pairings is a surprisingly good value.

Nobu Lanai

Four Seasons Resort Lanai, Manele Bay, 1 Manele Bay Road; tel: 808-565 4580; www.noburestaurants.com/lanai; $$$

Of all the Nobu restaurants around the world, this one has the most spectacular view – of Manele Bay and the Pacific Ocean. Sushi and sashimi here are as fresh as they come, while hot items – especially steak dishes – are also worth a try. Reservations essential.

Kauai

Art Café Hemingway

4-1495 Kuhio Highway, Kapa'a; tel: 808-822 2250; www.artcafehemingway.com; $

What do you get when you mix a historic building with an Eastern European menu and homage to Ernest Hemingway? This café, which also displays work from local artists. Locals rave about the food and rant about the service.

Bar Acuda

5-5161 Kuhio Highway, Hanalei; tel: 808-826 7081; www.restaurantbaracuda.com; $$$

Tapas (small plates), such as whole-roasted tomato bruschetta and Spanish chorizo with grilled apples, rule the menu at this unpretentious eatery in downtown Hanalei. Grab a seat on the tiny patio to dine under the stars.

Beach House

5022 Lawai Road, Koloa; tel: 808-742 1424; www.the-beach-house.com; $$$

Many say this is Kauai's best seafood restaurant – the lemongrass and kaffir-lime sea scallops are a local favorite. The setting is also stunning, especially at sunset. Vegetarian menu available. Reservations essential.

Brennecke's Beach Broiler

2100 Ho'one Road, Poipu; tel: 808-742 7588; www.brenneckes.com; $$

Portions are huge at this casual, busy bar with windows overlooking the beach. Burgers come with a veritable pile of fries and rib racks are longer than most human forearms. If you pre-

fer just drinks, there are two Happy Hours every day (3–5pm and 8.30pm until closing).

Caffe Coco

4-369 Kuhio Highway, Kapa'a; tel: 808-822 7990; $$

This café, in a restored plantation set back from the highway, serves up an eclectic menu that includes pot-stickers, samosas, Greek salads, fresh fish and soups. In nice weather, try to grab a seat in the garden out back.

Casa di Amici

2360 Nalo Road, Poipu; tel: 808-742 1555; www.casadiamici.com/menu.html; $$$

Classical piano music on Saturday nights makes the 'House of Friends' a popular romantic destination. The food certainly packs them in too; chefs make their own sausages, and risotto dishes that incorporate island produce never fail to impress. Children's menu available.

Hanama'ulu Restaurant, Tea House, Sushi Bar, and Robatayaki

3-4291 Kuhio Highway, Hanama'ulu; tel: 808-245 2511; $

Tearooms featuring tatami-seating are the highlight of this no-frills, pan-Asian restaurant that has added to its list of expertise over the years. Popular dishes include ginger chicken, fried shrimp and the robatayaki, which, essentially, comprises grilled meat and fish.

The terrace at Nobu Lanai

Keoki's Paradise
2360 Kiahuna Plantation Drive, Koloa; tel: 808-742 7534; www.keokisparadise.com; $$$
Food is almost secondary at this raucous restaurant, which is built to look like a Polynesian boathouse and boasts live music every night. Still, the list of seafood appetizers is always a good bet after a long day.

Postcards Café
5-5075A Kuhio Highway, Hanalei; tel: 808-826 1191; www.postcardscafe. com; $$
There really are postcards adorning the walls of this Hanalei café, which caters to vegans, vegetarians and meat-eaters alike. A local favorite: taro fritters, which often appear on the menu as a special. All deserts are made without refined sugar.

Restaurant Kintaro
4-370 Kuhio Highway, Wailua; tel: 808-822 3341; $$
Tatami-mat seating is available at this Japanese restaurant that is a favorite among locals. Try the Bali Hai bomb, a roll of crab and smoked salmon, baked and topped with wasabi mayonnaise. Expect long lines on weekends.

Tahiti Nui Restaurant and Cocktail Lounge
5-5134 Kuhio Highway, Hanalei; tel: 808-826 6277; www.thenui.com; $$
This Polynesian-themed restaurant and bar saw a huge spike in business after its star turn in *The Descendants*, the 2011 movie with George Clooney. There's live music nightly with Hawaiian slack-key guitar on Fridays.

Maui

Casanova Bistro
33 Lono Avenue, Kahului; tel: 808-873 3650; www.casanovamaui.com; $$–$$$
This smart Italian place in Kahului is the sister restaurant of Casanova Italian Restaurant (see page 83) in Makawao, an upcountry institution. The menu features delicious salads and pasta dishes, and a selection of meat and fish mains. Tapas is also served from 3pm daily.

Flatbread Company
89 Hana Highway; tel: 808-579 8989; www.flatbreadcompany.com; $$
Locals line up in droves for the brick-oven pizzas made with organic ingredients from this down-home restaurant just outside of downtown Paia. Vegetarians, rejoice: there are a number of meat-free pizzas and salads that are tremendous. Go early or expect a short to moderate wait at peak hours.

Grandma's Coffee House
9232 Kula Highway, Kula; tel: 808-878 2792; www.grandmascoffee.com; $
Yes, they sell coffee at this country-style restaurant on the Back Road to Hana, but the place is famous for

Baristas give a 'shaka' at Grandma's Coffee House

its giant breakfast dishes and its baked goods. On weekends there is live music on the small patio (in the shade of coffee plants).

Hula Grill

2435 Ka'apanali Parkway, Ka'anapali; tel: 808-667 6636; www.hulagrill.com; $$–$$$

This restaurant cranks out upscale pub food Hawaiian-style; think *pupus*, hamburgers and workmanlike fish dishes. Perhaps the best part of the eatery is the Barefoot Bar, with its live music and drink specials during Happy Hour on weekdays.

Ko

Fairmont Kea Lani, 4100 Wailea Alanui Drive; tel: 808-669 6299; http://ko restaurant.com; $$$$

This upscale Asian restaurant is the only place on Maui serving food inspired by Hawai'i's sugar cane plantation era, with dishes such as zarzuela and 'ono pulehu chicken. What's more, chef Tylun Pang incorporates family recipes from his own family and families of his line cooks. Reservations essential.

Honokowai Okazuya

3600-D Lower Honoapi'ilani Highway, Honokowai; tel: 808-665 0512; $

Locals swear by this hole-in-the-wall restaurant, located in a Honokowai strip mall. The signature dish: mahi-mahi with lemon capers, which always comes with a scoop of macaroni salad. The restaurant has a few small tables but is designed mostly for take-away.

Lahaina Grill

127 Lahainaluna Road, Lahaina; tel: 808-667 5117; $$$

Iconic chef David Paul is no longer associated with this upscale restaurant, but the food is still delicious. An obvious favorite is the Cake Walk, with samples of Kona lobster crab cake, Louisiana rock shrimp cake and seared ahi cake. Reservations essential.

Mala Ocean Tavern

1307 Front Street; tel: 808-667 9394; www.malaoceantavern.com; $$–$$$

This tiny restaurant overlooking the Mala Ramp and Lahaina Harbor offers an eclectic menu that touches on the Mediterranean, Italy, Thailand and the Middle East. If you can't sit on the patio, ask for a seat at the bar.

Mama's Fish House

799 Poho Place, on the highway near Paia; tel: 808-579 8488; www.mamasfishhouse.com; $$$$

It's no fluke that this has become Maui's most famous restaurant. The food – freshly caught fish from around the islands – is stellar and the beach-front view never ceases to amaze. The $16 Mai Tai is worth every cent, as is the fish curry with opah and ahi is recommended. It's also a great place to spot local celebs such as Sammy Hagar and Steven Tyler.

Seafood at Mama's Fish House

Manoli's Pizza Company

100 Wailea Ike Drive; tel: 808-874 7499; www.manolispizzacompany.com; $$–$$$

The gluten-free crust is a huge hit at this brick-oven pizzeria in Wailea, as it is one of the only pizza shops on the island to offer such an option. Menu options also include traditional pizzas and a host of homemade pastas. Delivery available.

Milagro's Food Company

3 Baldwin Avenue; tel: 808-579 8755; www.milagrosfoodcompany.com; $$

Margaritas and Tex-Mex food are the attractions at this closet-sized eatery near the intersection of Baldwin Avenue and the Hana Highway. Most ingredients are organic and some are even grown locally. Grab a seat on the patio and watch the world go by.

Plantation House Restaurant

2000 Plantation Club Drive, Kapalua; tel: 808-669 6299; www.theplantationhouse. com; $$$

Views of Molokai from this top-notch restaurant in the clubhouse on Kapalua's Plantation golf course are remarkable. The food is good too; chefs incorporate local produce and products into a modern take on traditional Hawaiian cuisine. Reservations essential.

Spago

Four Seasons Resort, 3900 Wailea Alanui Drive; www.fourseasons.com/maui/ dining/restaurants/spago; tel: 808-879 2999; $$$

Wolfgang Puck's famous restaurant translates well in Hawai'i, where chefs prepare freshly caught fish every night. Dessert is a spectacle, as well, with options such as passionfruit crème brûlée. In winter, Puck himself might be working the line. The Asian-inspired setting offers spectacular oceans views. Reservations essential.

Sansei Seafood Restaurant & Sushi Bar

600 Office Road, Kapalua; tel: 808-669-6286; $$$

There is sushi on Maui, and then there's Sansei. This cult favorite serves up a variety of traditional sushi dishes, as well as new spins that incorporate ingredients such as panko-flakes, Asian shrimp cakes and mango. Meat-based dishes are available, too.

Star Noodle

286 Kupuohi Street, Lahaina; tel: 808-667 5400; www.starnoodle.com; $

Disregard the location of this restaurant (in the Lahaina Light Industrial Park), as the food here is among the best on the island. Try the pan-roasted Brussels sprouts with bacon and *kim chee* purée, or the Lahaina fried soup (*fat chow fun*), with ground pork and bean sprouts. For a more sociable experience, sit at the communal table in the center of the restaurant. There's also a full saki bar.

NIGHTLIFE

In Hawai'i, most bars and hotels host live music – you'll find Hawaiian music and local bands performing across the state. It's rare to find a dancing venue outside of Waikiki, but try your hotel concierge or front desk, as they do pop up, then close, rather regularly on neighbor islands. Check the websites of local newspapers for up-to-date listings.

Concerts and Theaters

George Kahumoku Jr.'s Slack Key Show

Napili Kai Beach Resort, Lahaina, Maui; tel: 808-669 3858; www.slackkeyshow.com

Grammy-winner George Kahumoku Jr. invites Hawai'i's most renowned slack-key musicians to join him and play every Wednesday in the Aloha Pavilion at Napili Kai. The show is incredibly intimate. And the talent is off the charts.

Kahilu Theatre

67-1186 Lindsey Road, Waimea; tel: 808-885 6868; www.kahilutheatre.org

This small-town theater serves as a gathering place for the community, and offers concerts, plays and educational opportunities, often paired with the observatories, many of which are headquartered in Waimea town.

Kauai Concert Association

3-1901 Kaumualii Highway, Lihu'e, Kauai; tel: 808-245 7464; www.kauai-concert.org

This non-profit group puts together a concert series every year at the Kauai Community College Performing Arts Center, and they always seem to attract a big-name artist or two.

Maui Arts and Cultural Center

One Cameron Way, Kahului; tel: 808-242 2787; www.mauiarts.org

Where all the headliners play on Maui, and also an outdoor concert venue for regular Hawaiian music and other performances under the evening sky.

Neil Blaisdell Center

777 Ward Avenue, Honolulu; tel: 808-768 5400; www.blaisdellcenter.com

Every headliner Hawai'i gets comes to the Neil Blaisdell Center. It's a bit dated, but situated over an ancient spring that feeds the moat full of koi surrounding it, which almost makes up for the rest of it. Also home to the Hawai'i Opera Theater.

Palace Theater

38 Haili Street, Hilo; tel: 808-934 7010; www.hilopalace.com

The Palace Theater in Hilo is not your typical movie theater. The historic building serves as a venue for music, plays and films, including seasonal classics like *The Rocky Horror Picture Show* each Halloween. It's best to go in the evening when the day cools, since there's no air conditioning.

Bars/Nightclubs

Charley's

142 Hana Highway, Paia, Maui; tel: 808-579 9453; www.charleysmaui.com

This classic dive bar is a favorite among local surfers. DJs play reggae and house music on weekends.

Duke's Barefoot Bar

3610 Rice Street, Lihu'e, Kauai; tel: 808-246 9599; www.dukeskauai.com

Happy Hours are 'Aloha Hours' at this lively beachside bar in Nawiliwili on Kauai's East Side. Weekend nights feature live music, as well.

Hula Grill

Whalers Village, 2435 Kaanapali Parkway, Lahaina, Maui; tel: 808-667 6636; www.hulagrillkaanapali.com

Mostly restaurant, but part bar, Hula's has some of the best local musicians and serves as one of the top night-time hot spots in West Maui. Come early and stick around if you'd like a table – it fills up fast, especially on weekends.

La Mariana Sailing Club

50 Sand Island Access Road, Honolulu; tel: 808-848 2800; www.lamarianasailingclub.com

Tucked away on Keehi Lagoon, this is the quintessential Tiki Bar. Blowfish are lamps, the musicians are blind and talented, and transient sailors are at the bar.

M Nightclub

500 Ala Moana Boulevard, Honolulu; tel: 808-529 0010; http://mnlhnl.com/

This hipster hot spot is one of the better spots for dancing in Honolulu. The crowd is young and very well-dressed, so put on your party clothes.

The Dragon Upstairs

1038 Nu'uanu Avenue, Honolulu; tel: 808-526 1411; www.thedragonupstairs.com

This Chinatown dive bar hosts live jazz performances almost every night of the week, and sometimes they mix it up with other local talent, too.

The Study

The Modern, Waikiki; tel: 808-943 5800; www.themodernstudy.com

Speakeasies are alive and well in the Pacific Islands, and this pricey-yet-hip hot spot, with its entrance hidden behind a bookcase in the lobby, is Exhibit A. Come early for a sundowner by the pool at the Modern, then dance the night away.

Surfer (The Bar)

Turtle Bay Resort, 57-091 Kamehameha Highway, Kahuku; tel: 808-293 6000

The only late night spot for most of the north shore, this is a fun spot for young travelers to mingle with the local residents and the professional surfing crowd.

Trees Lounge

440 Aleka Place; Kapa'a, Kauai; tel: 808-823 0600; www.treesloungekauai.com

Live music and late-night dancing characterize the scene at this off-the-beaten-path bar. Park in the Coconut Marketplace and enjoy the walk on a balmy night.

Roadside stand on Maui

A–Z

A

Addresses

On neighbor islands, cities are wide-spread, and on the smaller islands of Molokai and Lanai, there's only one zip code per island. Be wary when booking accommodations if you're looking to be in a certain area – just because it says the town name, doesn't mean it's in it. Always check a map, or if in doubt, call the hotel prior to booking online.

Age restrictions

The legal driving age in Hawai'i is 16, and while considered an adult at 18, drinking of alcoholic beverages is not allowed for anyone under 21 years old. Bars that also serve as restaurants generally allow minors in until a certain time of the evening – usually 9pm.

B

Budgeting

Broadly speaking, Hawai'i ranks at the expensive end of American vacation destinations. Prices are generally high, as so much of what is consumed in the islands has to be shipped there from across the Pacific or beyond. In addition, many tourists are happy to pay premium rates for a once-in-a-lifetime holiday in paradise. However, it is possible to keep costs down. The finest hotels tend to charge at least $250 per room per night, and often double that. For pretty good accommodations close to the sea, it's perfectly possible to pay $125–150 in a hotel, or perhaps $100 for a rented condo.

The average visitor spends about $30 per day on food and drink; even if you buy and prepare your own meals, it's hard to go much lower than say $20 per day, while at the other end of the spectrum there are plenty of fine-dining restaurants charging $50 or more for a single meal. Average beers cost anywhere from $3 to $5 per pint; the average glass of house wine ranges from $6 to $12 (or $15 at posh restaurants).

You'll never have to pay to go on the beach and will rarely have to pay to access the islands' best hiking trails. Still, prices for most kinds of commercial activity – a snorkel- or whale-watching cruise, a bus tour, a submarine ride, a guided hike or bike ride – also tend to be high.

C

Children

Unless otherwise specified (or unless you're heading to a bar), most places in the Hawaiian Islands are child-friendly and actually encourage families to visit together. Many restaurants have children's menus and offer young kids crayons when they sit down. Many attractions

Fun for all the family on Waikiki Beach

charge reduced-price admission fees for children. Also, most luxury hotels will recommend babysitting services.

Private and independent babysitting services exist on every island and many travelers use them without incident.

Clothing

In Hawai'i, attire is almost always casual. While the downtown working crowd dresses a bit nicer, it's rare you'll see a suit. For the rest of residents, shorts and T-shirts and sundresses are the norm. Jeans are always appropriate for evenings out, and only at the most fancy of restaurants will closed-toe shoes be required. Some do, however, require a collared shirt or no tank tops in the evening, so if going somewhere nice, call ahead. In Waikiki, you'll sometimes see visitors walking around in only a swimsuit. While it's almost always warm enough to do so, it's considered polite to cover up – so throw on a shirt or sarong before leaving the beach to go shop or eat.

You're likely to encounter rain at some point during your stay, so you'll be glad of light, waterproof clothing or perhaps an umbrella. If you plan to venture at all higher, to areas like Maui's Upcountry, you'll need something warmer too. And if you head towards the summits of the volcanoes, most notably for the dawn at Haleakala on Maui, you should be prepared for literally freezing temperatures.

All the islands hold rough volcanic terrain, so good walking shoes or hiking boots are very useful, and in many places the ocean floor can be rocky and abrasive, so reef shoes are a good idea too.

Crime and safety

Hawai'i has earned a reputation for hospitality and all the good cheer that the word *aloha* implies. However, travelers should be warned that all types of crime – including burglaries, robberies, assaults and rapes – do occur on the islands. To avoid them, follow the usual precautions as when traveling anywhere else. If you're out late, it's best to travel in pairs. Use common sense. Don't carry jewelry, large amounts of cash, or other valuables. In areas far from population centers, car break-ins and beach thefts of unattended personal property are becoming common, even at popular tourist sites. Never leave valuables (or anything) visible in your car. If your hotel has a safe in the room, it is advisable to use it.

Customs

Travelers from the mainland United States to Hawai'i are not eligible for duty-free shopping, but travelers from other nations are. There is no limit to the amount of money travelers are allowed to bring into Hawai'i – or any part of the United States, for that matter – but any amount exceeding $10,000 requires a formal report with US Customs.

In order to prevent the spread of fruit flies and other hazardous plant insects and disease, no fruit, plants or live snails from the mainland are allowed

Slippers, essential footwear in Hawai'i

into Hawai'i, and no fruit, plants or live snails from Hawai'i are allowed to be brought back to the mainland.

D

Disabled travelers

Hawai'i is very well geared towards meeting the needs of disabled travelers. Download detailed reports on facilities from the website of the State of Hawai'i Disability and Communication Access Board (tel: 808-586 8121; http://health.hawaii.gov/dcab). Specific information on Hawaiian hotels is also available from Access-Able (www.access-able.com). Many vehicles on public transportation networks on Oahu and Maui are adapted for travelers with disabilities.

E

Electricity

Standard US 110-120 volts, 60 cycles AC. Large hotels usually are able to provide voltage and plug converters, so you only need to bring one if renting a condo or smaller B&B.

Embassies and consulates

There aren't many embassies in Hawai'i – most of the formal diplomatic outposts are on the mainland, in Los Angeles, or in San Francisco. Still, the islands are home to a number of consulates:
Australia, tel: 808-524 5050
Japan, tel: 808-543 3111
Korea, tel: 808-595 6109

Philippines, tel: 808-595 6316
Taiwan, tel: 808-595 6347

Emergencies

Hawai'i has its own response units, and outposts of major national responders as well. In the event of emergencies, there are a number of options to call for help:
American Red Cross, tel: 808-734 2101
Coast Guard Search and Rescue, tel: 800-552 6458
Dental emergency service, tel: 808-944 8863
Fire, Police, Ambulance, tel: 911
Lifeguard service, tel: 808-922 3888
Poison Center, tel: 808-941 4411

Etiquette

All etiquette rules for the mainland United States apply to the Hawaiian Islands as well. In addition, it is custom in Hawai'i to remove shoes before entering someone's private home – a little bit of Japanese culture that has taken off in Hawai'i.

Note that islanders can be lax about time, especially when going on dates and to meetings outside of strictly commercial business circles. This habit of being late by 10 to 20 minutes is generally known as being on 'Hawaiian time' and doesn't mean the person doesn't respect your time, it's just part of the slower pace of Hawai'i.

Tipping for service is expected in Hawai'i, as tips are considered part of a service worker's overall salary. In general, airport porters' baggage-handling

An Aloha Festival

fees run at roughly $1 per bag, and taxi drivers are usually tipped 10 percent in addition to about 25¢ per bag. A 15–20 percent tip at a fine restaurant is the norm, and at other eating establishments you should tip whatever you feel is fair, typically 15 percent.

F

Festivals

For such a relatively small state, Hawai'i has a host of festivals throughout the year, some of which are more tourist-friendly than others. For an up-to-date calendar visit www.gohawaii.com.

The largest and perhaps most exciting for visitors are the Merrie Monarch Festival each April (Hilo, www.merriemonarch festival.org); May Day festivals, which happen statewide May 1 and celebrate lei in Hawai'i; Chinese New Year, usually occurring late January and most exciting in Honolulu's Chinatown; Punahou Carnival and the 50th State Fair, which are both family-fun events with rides, occurring in February and June, respectively; and Aloha Festivals, a series of statewide, month-long celebrations encompassing beautiful floral parades, street parties, special ceremonies, and community events to celebrate the spirit of *aloha* each September (www.aloha festivals.com). Others worth attending, depending upon your particular interests, include the Kapalua Wine & Food Festival each June on Maui (www.kapaluawine andfoodfestival.com); the statewide Bon Odori Dance Festivals, evening events in which visitors are invited to join; and the Hawai'i International Film Festival on Oahu each November, an acclaimed two-week festival featuring international films and celebrating an 'East meets West' theme (www.hiff.org).

G

Gay and lesbian travelers

Hawai'i always has been a popular spot among gay and lesbian travelers, and the destination became even more gay-friendly when the state legislature legalized same-sex marriage in 2013. Since this historic change, many accommodations have added gay-friendly packages and special deals for same-sex couples seeking to plan destination weddings. Some of the properties that were gay friendly before the new law include the Waikiki Grand Hotel on Oahu (www. castleresorts.com), the Sunseeker Resort on Maui (www.mauisunseeker. com) and the Mahina Kai B&B on Kauai (www.mahinakai.com).

H

Health

Inoculations
No additional inoculations are required prior to travel to Hawai'i.

Health care and insurance
It is always prudent to take out travel insurance that covers medical issues

Kamehameha Day Statue

there is no free health care in the United States.

Doctors, pharmacies and hospitals

Most of the larger hotels have a physician on call. Other medical services can be obtained at hospitals and/or clinics, which are prevalent on every island except Lanai. At bigger hospitals, the quality of care is superb. At some of the smaller clinics and medical outposts, care may be less so. There are emergency walk-in clinics, known as minute clinics, in many local pharmacies.

For prescription medicine, there are pharmacies located in most towns around the islands. In larger towns, at least one pharmacy is usually open 24 hours. It will be the closest Longs (on Kalakaua if you're in Waikiki) or Walgreens.

Pharmacies only are necessary to fill prescriptions; all supermarkets (and many corner markets) in the United States sell a sampling of over-the-counter medications.

Hours and holidays

Because Hawai'i is so attuned to its visitors, shops and restaurants in high-traffic tourist areas like Waikiki, Ka'anapali, Kona and Lihu'e are open 365 days a year. Expect to see some closures on Thanksgiving (the 4th Thursday of November) and Christmas Day – but usually only in the late afternoon and evening.

In general, stores are open for shopping by 9am and lunch restaurants are open by 11am.

Hawai'i observes all the US national holidays, plus three state holidays – Prince Kuhio Day, Kamehameha Day and Admission Day. On national holidays, all government offices, banks, post offices and most businesses – except shops – close. On state holidays, local government offices and banks close, but federal offices and post offices remain open. Here are the important holidays to note:

New Year's Day: January 1
Martin Luther King Day: third Monday in January
Presidents' Day: third Monday in February
Prince Kuhio Day: March 26
Good Friday: Friday preceding Easter Sunday
Memorial Day: last Monday in May
Kamehameha Day: June 11
Independence Day: July 4
Admission Day: third Friday in August
Labor Day: first Monday in September
Columbus Day: October 12
Veterans Day: November 11
Thanksgiving Day: fourth Thursday in November
Christmas Day: December 25

Internet facilities

Internet access is widely available throughout Hawai'i. Upscale hotels

invariably offer high-speed access from guest rooms (though usually for a fee of anywhere from $10 to $15 per day), while most resorts offer free Wi-Fi in their respective lobbies. Free Wi-Fi also is available at most coffee shops. All state libraries and most university libraries provide free access and these days, a number of other types of commercial enterprises – from restaurants to boutiques – also offer free Wi-Fi.

L

Language

English is the most commonly spoken language, although Hawaiian and Pidgin English, a dialect, are both heard as well. Hawaiian language has experienced a major renaissance in the past 20 years, and has gone from almost obsolete to being offered in all of the schools and as a major at University of Hawai'i. Pidgin can be a bit tricky to pick up, but you'll get a knack for it after listening to the locals. However, don't try to imitate it, as it makes the locals laugh at you.

M

Media

Newspapers

Hawai'i has a handful of island daily and weekly newspapers. On Oahu, the main daily is the *Honolulu Star-Advertiser*; this is the de facto daily for other islands as well. Neighbor islands also have their own daily newspapers, with circulation restricted to that specific island. These papers publish wire copy about state and national stories, but have the feeling of community newspapers (because their respective readerships are so small). A variety of other newspapers are published by ethnic groups, the military, religious organizations, and by the tourism and business industries. On Maui, *Maui Time* has amassed quite a following for the way it covers entertainment news. The Associated Press maintains a bureau in Honolulu to cover both Hawai'i and the areas around the Pacific.

Radio

Honolulu's listeners have some 30 radio stations to listen to; there are fewer stations elsewhere on Oahu and on other islands. Hawai'i Public Radio news and fine arts can be found on KHPR 88.1 in Honolulu; KKUA 90.7 on Maui, Molokai, and Lanai; and KANO 91.1 in Hilo. Hawai'i Public Radio talk and music can be found on KIPO 89.3 in Honolulu; KIPM 89.7 on Maui, Molokai and Lanai; and KIPL 89.9 on Kauai. ESPN sports radio is KKEA 1420 AM. KHUI (99.5 FM) and KINE (105.1 FM), both in Honolulu, broadcast both contemporary and traditional Hawaiian music. Listings in the local newspapers give relevant frequencies.

Television

There are more than 10 broadcast television channels that originate in the state of Hawai'i. For broadcasts originating on Oahu (in Honolulu), relay trans-

Offerings at a heiau site, Kawaihae

mitters serve the neighbor islands, while private companies provide cable TV programming by subscription only. Most of the other islands have their own local access channels. The majority of moderate-to-good hotels offer cable viewing to guests, showing a vast array of channels and, in a separate facility, first-run movies.

Money

Hawai'i uses standard US currency and coins in all denominations. $1 = 100 cents. All major credit cards are accepted, including American Express, Visa, MasterCard and Discover. Most car rental companies require a credit card. Cash machines (ATMs) are everywhere, especially at banks and shopping centers; ATMs accept bank cards from the mainland (and abroad) and are accessible 24 hours a day.

Currency exchange

Currency conversion is readily available at all of the state's international airports, and at most major banks. Currency exchange is also available at most hotels, although the rate tends to be a little less favorable than at a bank. There are no street money changers in Hawai'i.

P

Post

Believe it or not, normal American postal rates apply across Hawai'i. From Honolulu, it costs the same price to mail a letter to New York City as it does to Maui.

Stamps are sold at all post offices; most supermarkets and corner stores sell them, too, and ATMs even carry them. Post boxes in Hawai'i look the same as they do across the mainland US – blue boxes with an arched top.

Most resort hotels will mail postcards with postage affixed free of charge.

R

Religion

Hawai'i's most common religion is Christianity, however, there are a great deal of other religions alive and actively practiced in Hawai'i. Tolerance is very high for all religions – Hawai'i is a melting pot, after all. Religion is rarely talked about and is considered very personal, so if speaking to the locals, wait for them to bring it up, if at all.

Traditional Hawaiian cultural practices are on the rise with the rebirth of the culture, although there are not many who identify solely with this as their religion.

S

Smoking

Smoking is generally considered taboo in Hawai'i – one can't smoke in any bars or restaurants, nor in hotels or public recreation areas. The age requirement for buying tobacco was recently raised from 18 to 21, and smoking is banned on all public beaches (which is all beaches, really). A violation includes a ticket and fine.

Sunset on the summit of Mauna Kea

If stepping outside of a restaurant or other business to smoke, be sure to move a minimum of 20ft (6 meters) from any doorway or window.

T

Telephones

From the middle of the Pacific, you can dial directly to almost anywhere in the world. Because of underwater fiber-optic cables, the quality of phone calls to both Asia and North America is excellent. Cellular service is reliable as well; major carriers servicing the Hawaiian Islands include AT&T, Verizon, Sprint and T-Mobile, and all of them sell pay-as-you-go plans for international travelers. If you prefer dialing out from a hotel, note that most hotels charge $0.75–1 for local calls, and up to $1 per minute for long distance. If you can find public telephones (most of them have been phased out), they cost $0.35 per minute for local calls.

Area and dialing codes

The telephone area code for all the Hawaiian Islands is **808**.

Same-island calls:
dial number. Note that 800 numbers need to be preceeded by a 1, i.e. 1 + 800 + number.

Inter-island (direct):
1 + 808 + number.

Mainland (direct dial):
1 + area code + number.

International (direct dial):
011 + country + city + number.

Home-country direct:
Operators in some countries can be called directly from Hawai'i by special toll-free 800 numbers. Call 643-1000 for a list of numbers and foreign countries where this particular service is available.

Time zones

Hawai'i is GMT-10 hours, which means it is 10 hours behind Greenwich Mean Time, two hours behind Pacific Standard Time, three hours behind Mountain Standard Time, four hours behind Central Standard Time and five hours behind Eastern Standard Time. As Hawai'i does not adjust to Daylight Saving Time, these time differences grow by one hour between April and October (or, some years, November).

Toilets

Toilets in Hawai'i are standard Western toilets, although occasionally, in higher-end resorts, you may find Japanese-style toilets. These are similar to Western toilets but with many added buttons, bells and whistles.

Public toilets can be hard to find in urban areas – most shops won't let you use theirs. However, restaurants usually have one, and state beach parks do as well.

Tourist information

The Hawai'i Visitors and Conventions Bureau is in charge of promoting Hawai'i to the general public. While the majority of the organization's efforts focus on media and corporate tourism, the website can be useful (www.gohawaii.com)

Tours and guides

Many US-based tour operators offer tours in Hawai'i that are available to customers from anywhere in the world; the most useful include **Backroads** (tel: 800-462 2848; www.backroads.com), **Roberts Hawai'i** (tel: 800-831 5541; www.robertshawaii.com), **Pleasant Hawaiian Holidays** (tel: 800-742 9244; www.pleasantholidays.com), the **Sierra Club** (tel: 415-977 5522; www.sierra-club.org), and **Tauck Tours** (tel: 800-788 7885; www.tauck.com). For a truly local experience on Oahu, choose the small group tours of Keawe Adventures (www.keaweadventures.com), run by a local native Hawaiian offering diverse services – everything from a guided tour of the USS *Arizona* to fly fishing, and the first choice of visiting celebrities.

Transportation

Arrival by air

Hawai'i is regularly serviced from the US mainland, Canada, Europe, the South Pacific and Asia. Flying time is about 10 hours from New York, eight hours from Chicago, and five hours from Los Angeles. The Hawaiian Islands also are a major stopover point for flights traveling between the US mainland and Asia, Australia and New Zealand.

Oahu

It might be Hawai'i's most populous island but Oahu only has one commercial airport, **Honolulu International Airport** (tel: 808-836 6411; www.hawaii.gov/hnl). However, over the years this has become one of the busiest airports in the entire US, with over 21 million passengers each year. In addition to the main terminal building, the airport operates two other terminals: the inter-island terminal and the commuter-airline terminal. The airport operates a free shuttle system between these buildings from 6am to 10pm, but it's only a 10–15 minute walk if you're up for stretching your legs and have time.

Maui

Maui has three airports. The main one, **Kahului Airport** (tel: 808-872 3830; www.hawaii.gov/ogg), handles a growing number of direct flights from the US mainland and many inter-island hops. The two other airports, the **Kapalua-West Maui Airport** (tel: 808-665 6108; www.hawaii.gov/jhm) and **Hana Airport** (tel: 808-248 4861; www.hawaii.gov/hnm), are significantly smaller; both are served by inter-island Flying to Hana from one of the other Maui airports is an efficient option if you don't want to drive the Hana Highway.

Hawai'i Island

Hawai'i Island has two main airports, **Kona International Airport** at Keahole (tel: 808-327 9520; www.hawaii.gov/koa) on the popular west side, and **Hilo International Airport** (tel: 808-961 9300; www.hawaii.gov/ito) on the outskirts of Hilo.

Cruise ship off the Napali Coast

Kauai

On Kauai, **Lihu'e Airport** (tel: 808-246 1448) has direct flights daily from San Francisco and Los Angeles on the US mainland, as well as numerous inter-island flights from Honolulu and other neighboring island airports. It is the smallest of all the airports on the four major Hawaiian Islands.

Molokai and Lanai

Molokai's Ho'olehua Airport tel: 808-567 9660; www.hawaii.gov/mkk) in south-central Molokai, handles inter-island flights only. The same is true at **Lanai Airport** (tel: 808-565 7942; www.hawaii.gov/lmn), 10 miles from Lanai City. For more information about aircraft that serve these destinations, visit www.hawaii.gov/dot/airports.

Arrival by boat

Numerous cruise ships including **Crystal Cruises** (www.crystalcruises.com), **Princess Cruises** (www.princess.com), and **Royal Caribbean** (www.royalcaribbean.com) now make Hawai'i a port of call, stopping in Honolulu as well as the neighbor islands as part of their itinerary. From the ports, taxis are your best bet for getting around.

Inter-island travel

Flights between islands are frequent, every half hour or hour. There is one primary carrier, **Hawaiian Airlines** (www.hawaiianairlines.com), which use jets between all major airports.

In addition, **Island Air** (www.islandair.com), uses small propeller craft to smaller airports such as the one near Princeville, on Kauai. There are also fixed-wing and helicopter flights for inter-island travel. **Mokulele Airlines** (www.mokuleleairlines.com) and **Pacific Wings** (www.pacificwings.com) are smaller airlines that offer small-plane flights from many of the major airports to smaller airports (such as Hana and Lanai). You can usually get a seat on one of these inter-island flights at short notice.

Public transportation

If you're staying on one island, the best option is to rent a car; it's cheaper than taking taxis everywhere and more reliable (and efficient) than public transportation. If you're island hopping, you'll either have to fly or take a ferry, though ferries only run between Maui, Lanai and Molokai.

Bus

All four of the major Hawaiian Islands (Oahu, Maui, Hawai'i Island and Kauai) have some form of mass transport. Depending on where you want to get to and how long you're willing to wait to get there, utilizing these systems may make sense during your visit.

The bus system on Oahu, dubbed **TheBus**, is the best in the state. This bus system covers the entire island, and the fare is the same regardless of whether you travel six blocks or all

Waikiki Trolley

the way around. TheBus is especially efficient in downtown Honolulu, with buses stopping every 15 minutes around Waikiki and the Ala Moana Shopping Center. Fares for TheBus are $2.50 per ride. Each ride includes one transfer, but you must ask the driver if you want a transfer ticket. Exact change is required and dollar bills are accepted. A four-day pass of unlimited rides costs $25 and is available at ABC convenience stores in downtown Honolulu. Important route numbers for Waikiki are 2, 4, 8, 19, 20, 58 and the City Express Route A. Route booklets listing other routes are available all over town.

The open-air **Waikiki Trolley** (tel: 808-591 2561; www.waikikitrolley. com) is another reliable option for getting around town. This system has four lines and makes dozens of stops. The Honolulu City Line (Red Line) travels between Waikiki and the Bishop Museum. The Ocean Coast Line (Blue Line), hugs Honolulu's southeastern coastline, including Diamond Head and Hanauma Bay. The Ala Moana Shuttle Line (Pink Line) stretches from the DFS Galleria Waikiki or Hilton Hawaiian Village to the Ala Moana Shopping Center. Finally, the Local Shopping & Dining Line (Yellow Line) starts at Ala Moana Center and stops at popular shopping destinations, including Ward Warehouse. A one-day, four-line ticket costs $30; four-day tickets (also good for all four lines)

cost $52. There are discounts when ordering online.

On Maui, there is the **Maui Bus** (tel: 808-871 4838; www.mauicounty.gov/ bus). Operated by Roberts Hawai'i, this system offers 10 routes between various communities. Two routes – the Upcountry and Haiku Islander routes – include a stop at Kahului Airport. Buses cover all of the island's major destinations, and fares are $2 per person.

On Hawai'i Island, the best bus option is the **Hele-On Bus** (tel: 808-961 8744; www.heleonbus.org), which covers all major towns and runs the four-hour trip from Kona to Hilo three times each day. Fares for this system are $1 per ride. Expect delays.

Kauai

On the Garden Isle, The Kauai Bus (tel: 808-246 8110; www.kauai.gov/transportation) runs hourly from Hanalei to Kakaha every day except Sunday. It also provides a midday shuttle around Lihu'e. Fares are $2 per ride.

Car

Most visitors to Hawai'i prefer to rent cars. This option provides travelers with the flexibility to go where they want, when they want. (On Molokai, renting a car is the only way to explore without the help of a tour outfitter.) It is also more affordable than taking taxis. Rates start at $25–35 per day for economy cars, and child car seats are an additional charge of $5–8 per day. All major car

A rugged section of the Hana Highway

rental companies operate in Hawai'i and many have 24-hour counters at most airports. Book in advance – or through online travel agents – for the best deals.

Drivers generally are required to be 25 years or older, have a valid driver's license (non-US license holders should check if their car rental company requires an international license) and a major credit card.

Driving

It is worth noting that driving in Hawai'i is much like driving on the US mainland. Traffic advances on the right side of the road, and it is legal to make right turns on red lights unless posted otherwise. All passengers must wear seatbelts and infants and young children must be strapped into car seats or booster seats as appropriate. Pedestrians, whether in a crosswalk or not, always have the right of way. Most roads are paved; highways are well maintained; signs are in English and/or international symbols; speed limits and distance are indicated almost exclusively in miles and miles-per-hour.

Taxis

Taxi service is available on all islands, including Lanai and Molokai. Rates vary from island to island; all taxis are metered, and most are available for sightseeing at a fixed rate. Honolulu, of course, has the most taxis, but don't expect to flag one down on the street. If a taxi is required, go to a nearby hotel.

There are dozens of cab companies on every island. On Oahu, try The CAB (tel: 808-422 2222; www.thecabhawaii. com). On Maui, use CB Taxi (tel: 808-243 8294; www.cbtaximaui.com). On Hawai'i Island, book with Laura's Taxi (tel: 808-326 5466; www.laurastaxi. com), and on Kauai, try Pono Taxi (tel: 808-634 4744; www.ponotaxi.com).

Visas and passports

Details of the visa waiver scheme, under which travelers carrying passports issued by Britain, Ireland and most European countries, as well as Australia and New Zealand, do not need visas for trips to the United States lasting less than 90 days, can be obtained from your travel agent or via http://travel.state.gov.

W

Weights and measures

Hawai'i uses the imperial system of weights and measures. Metric weights and measures are rarely used.

Women travelers

Women have equal rights in the United States – including Hawai'i. It's generally quite safe for women to travel alone, however, find company for late evenings out or hiking, to be sure.

BOOKS AND FILM

With lush valleys, waterfalls and tropical paradise around every corner, Hawai'i has become a darling of Hollywood and inspiration for writers. You can't really blame Hollywood producers for falling in love with Hawai'i, the islands offer a more authentic paradise than any studio set. More than 100 films have been shot in the islands since the 1950s, and countless other television shows have been filmed there, as well. Some islands, such as Kauai, are more famous than others.

Hawai'i has the ability to morph easily, making the audience believe it is anything from a South Pacific beach to a South African village to an exotic Peruvian rainforest. Tax breaks and other incentives help to attract Hollywood studios and film-makers.

When Hawai'i stars as Hawai'i, movies like *50 First Dates* and the book and film *The Descendents* capture it most authentically. For historical fiction, *Molokai* tells the story of Kalaupapa as a leper colony in a way you'll never forget.

Books

Non-Fiction

The Betrayal of Lili'uokalani by Helena G. Allen. All-important biography of Hawai'i's last queen.

Diamond Head, Hawai'i's Icon by Allan Seiden. A comprehensive look at Hawai'i's most renowned landmark.

Discovery by Bishop Museum Press. A superb collection of essays and photographs addressing ancient, contemporary and future Hawai'i.

Haleakala: A History of the Maui Mountain by Jill Engledow. A look at the science of how Haleakala was formed, as well as the people who live there today.

Hawai'i 1959–89 by Gavan Daws. A thorough history of Hawai'i's first 30 years of statehood.

Hawai'i's Story by Hawai'i's Queen by Queen Lili'uokalani. The memoirs of Hawai'i's first and only reigning queen.

Hawaiian Dictionary by Mary Kawena Pukui and Samuel H. Elbert. The definitive reference on Hawaiian vocabulary.

Hawaiian Legends by William Hyde Rice. Attractive reprint of a 1923 classic, with new photos by Boone Morrison.

Hawaiian Mythology by Martha Warren Beckwith. Definitive and comprehensive.

Mark Twain's Letters from Hawai'i. Twain's look at Hawai'i in the 1860s.

Volcanoes in the Sea by Gordon A. MacDonald. A historical and scientific look at Hawai'i's spectacular volcanoes.

Waikiki Beachboy by Grady Timmons. A colorful history of Waikiki's famed beachboy era.

Fiction

The Descendants by Kaui Hart Hemmings. The novel that inspired the motion picture of the same name; about

death, family bonding and land ownership in Hawai'i.

Fluke: Or I Know Why the Winged Whale Sings by Christopher Moore. This novel is based on humpback whale researchers who conduct work off the coast of Maui every winter.

From Here to Eternity by James Jones. The novel that spawned a movie (and a musical); tells the story of military life on Oahu leading up to the attack on Pearl Harbor in 1941.

Molokai by Alan Brennert. This historical fiction follows the life of a leper exiled to Moloka'i at age five.

Film

Waikiki Wedding, 1937. A musical starring the famous Bing Crosby that created two hit songs.

From Here to Eternity, 1953. Put the islands on the map and starred Burt Lancaster, Frank Sinatra, Montgomery Clift, and Deborah Kerr.

South Pacific, 1958. A musical set in war times, was largely filmed on the north shore of Kauai.

Blue Hawai'i, 1961. Elvis Presley made Hawai'i everyman's dream vacation with this musical comedy filmed on Kauai.

Girls! Girls! Girls!, 1962. followed up on the success of *Blue Hawai'i* and also starred Elvis Presley.

North Shore, 1987. A surf movie, showed the world that the North Shore of Oahu is the center of the surfing universe.

Jurassic Park, 1993. Part sci-fi, part drama, was largely filmed at Oahu's Kualoa Ranch, and is the story of an island attraction that features real life dinosaurs.

Waterworld, 1995. A sci-fi movie about a world without land, was filmed off the coast of the islands.

Outbreak, 1995. A movie about a medical disaster starring Dustin Hoffman, portrays Kauai as Africa in this film.

Six Days, Seven Nights, 1998. Features Hawai'i as a desert island that Harrison Ford and Anne Heche must survive together on.

Pearl Harbor, 2001. A dramatic telling of the attack on Pearl Harbor, filmed largely onsite at Pearl Harbor Naval Base.

Pirates of the Caribbean, 2003. This film launched the million-dollar series starring Johnny Depp with a movie filmed largely in the islands.

50 First Dates, 2004. Filmed at Sea Life Park on Oahu, is a Drew Barrymore and Adam Sandler comedy.

Forgetting Sarah Marshall, 2008. A romantic comedy starring Jason Segel and Kristin Bell, was filmed almost exclusively at Turtle Bay Resort.

Rise of Planet of the Apes, 2011. Filmed partly in Hawai'i, is a prequel to the famous *Planet of the Apes*.

The Descendants, 2011. The most real depiction of life in Hawai'i, written by local author Kaui Hart Hemmings, features George Clooney and many familiar Oahu and Kauai sights.

Aloha, 2015. This James Cameron rom-com/drama depicts interactions between Hawai'i's military and local residents.

ABOUT THIS BOOK

This *Explore Guide* has been produced by the editors of Insight Guides, whose books have set the standard for visual travel guides since 1970. With top-quality photography and authoritative recommendations, these guidebooks bring you the very best routes and itineraries in the world's most exciting destinations.

BEST ROUTES

The routes in the book provide something to suit all budgets, tastes and trip lengths. As well as covering the destination's many classic attractions, the itineraries track lesser-known sights, and there are also excursions for those who want to extend their visit outside the city. The routes embrace a range of interests, so whether you are an art fan, a gourmet, a history buff or have kids to entertain, you will find an option to suit.

We recommend reading the whole of a route before setting out. This should help you to familiarise yourself with it and enable you to plan where to stop for refreshments – options are shown in the 'Food and Drink' box at the end of each tour.

For our pick of the tours by theme, consult Recommended Routes for… (see pages 6–7).

INTRODUCTION

The routes are set in context by this introductory section, giving an overview of the destination to set the scene, plus background information on food and drink, shopping and more, while a succinct history timeline highlights the key events over the centuries.

DIRECTORY

Also supporting the routes is a Directory chapter, with a clearly organised A–Z of practical information, our pick of where to stay while you are there and select restaurant listings; these eateries complement the more low-key cafés and restaurants that feature within the routes and are intended to offer a wider choice for evening dining. Also included here are some nightlife listings and our recommendations for books and films about the destination.

ABOUT THE AUTHORS

Rachel Ross is a freelance writer who grew up in Honolulu, Hawai'i, and writes for local and national publications about things to do in her beloved home state. She has traveled each of the islands extensively and discovers something new to write about each time. This book builds on content originally written by Scott Rutherford.

CONTACT THE EDITORS

We hope you find this Explore Guide useful, interesting and a pleasure to read. If you have any questions or feedback on the text, pictures or maps, please do let us know. If you have noticed any errors or outdated facts, or have suggestions for places to include on the routes, we would be delighted to hear from you. Please drop us an email at hello@insightguides.com. Thanks!

REDITS

Explore Hawaii
Editor: Rachel Lawrence
Author: Rachel Ross
Head of Production: Rebeka Davies
Picture Editor: Tom Smyth
Cartography: original cartography
Berndtson & Berndtson, updated by Carte
Photo Credits: 123RF 42; Alamy 109,
122, 123; Barbara Kraft/Four Seasons 99,
104/105; Disney Enterprises 45, 88; Don
Riddle/Four Seasons 101; Four Seasons
93; Getty Images 4/5T, 27, 30/31, 42/43,
52, 63L, 65, 66/67, 68, 118/119; Hawaii
Tourism Authority/Dana Edmunds 18/19,
86MR, 112, 115; Hawaii Tourism Authority/
Joe Solem 114; Hawaii Tourism Authority/Tor
Johnson 8ML, 16, 17L, 23, 33L, 32/33, 73,
75, 86MR, 86MC, 98, 108, 113, 116; iStock
4MC, 7T, 14/15; Leonardo 22, 91, 96, 102;
Public domain 26; Roy's 100; Shutterstock
64, 74; Starwood Hotels & Resorts 18,
86/87T, 86ML, 86MC, 86ML, 89, 90, 94,
95, 97; Steven Greaves/Apa Publications 1,
4ML, 4MC, 4MR, 6TL, 6MC, 6ML, 7MR, 7M,
7MR, 8MC, 8ML, 8MC, 8MR, 8MR, 8/9T, 10,
11, 12, 13L, 12/13, 16/17, 19L, 20, 21L,
24, 25L, 24/25, 28ML, 28MC, 28MR, 28ML,
28MC, 28MR, 28/29T, 32T, 37L, 39, 40, 41L,
40/41, 44T, 46, 49L, 50, 51, 53, 54, 55L,
54/55, 56, 57, 58, 59, 60, 61B, 61T, 62,
62/63, 69, 70, 71L, 70/71, 72, 76, 77, 78,
79L, 78/79, 80, 81L, 80/81, 82, 83, 84, 85,
92, 103, 106, 107, 110, 111, 117, 120, 121;
Tim Thompson/Apa Publications 4MR, 4ML,
6BC, 20/21, 32B, 34B, 34T, 35, 36, 36/37,
38, 43L, 44B, 47L, 46/47, 48, 48/49
Cover credits: Shutterstock (main & BL)

Printed by CTPS – China

First Edition 2016
All Rights Reserved
© 2016 Apa Digital (CH) AG and
Apa Publications (UK) Ltd

DISTRIBUTION

UK, Ireland and Europe
Apa Publications (UK) Ltd
sales@insightguides.com
United States and Canada
Ingram Publisher Services
ips@ingramcontent.com
Southeast Asia
Woodslane
info@woodslane.com.au
Australia and New Zealand
Apa Publications (Singapore) Pte
singaporeoffice@insightguides.com
Hong Kong, Taiwan and China
Apa Publications (HK) Ltd
hongkongoffice@insightguides.com
Worldwide
Apa Publications (UK) Ltd
sales@insightguides.com

SPECIAL SALES, CONTENT LICENSING AND COPUBLISHING

Insight Guides can be purchased in bulk
quantities at discounted prices. We can
create special editions, personalised
jackets and corporate imprints tailored to
your needs.
sales@insightguides.com
www.insightguides.biz

INDEX

MAP LEGEND

●	Start of tour
→	Tour & route direction
❶	Recommended sight
❷	Recommended restaurant/café
★	Place of interest
❶	Tourist information
✈	Airport
🚌	Main bus station
✉	Post office
▯	Statue/monument
Ⓜ	Museum/gallery
📖	Library
🎭	Theatre
✚	Hospital
⛪	Church
⚲	Buddhist temple
🗼	Lighthouse
☊	Cave
⚑	Beach
⛺	Campsite
✳	Viewpoint
2713 △	Altitude in ft
▮	Important building
▯	Urban area
▯	Park
▯	Non-urban area